CONTENTS

Silent Suffering

Finding God's Faithfulness in Chronic Lyme Disease

Lauren Murphree

DEDICATION

To Andy, my love. Nobody knows how mu
behind the scenes to take care of me and lov
so honored to be your wife and humbled th
me you to walk through this life with. Tha
representing Jesus to me on some of my wor
you, forever and always.

And to everyone struggling with chronic illn
not forgotten. You are loved. What you've wa
has not gone unnoticed. May God grant you
and so much more. May you live in abundanc
entire being – heart, body, mind, and soul be
healed - in Jesus name.

"Speak up for those who cannot speak for themselves, for the rights of all who are destitute. Speak up and judge fairly; defend the rights of the poor and needy."
Proverbs 31:8-9 (NIV)

ACKNOWLEDGMENTS

There are hundreds and hundreds of people (too many to count!) to thank on a deep level. So, to all the people who have supported me in any way: I would not be where I am today without each of you and your support. May God bless every single one of you - abundantly.

To name a few: Meag and Eric, Stacey and Ed, Guy Murphree, the Campbells, Kelsey Tichenor, the pink house ladies, Holly Alyea, Dawn Grigor, Gudrun, the Cundy family, the Furhmans, Aaron Yu, the Ortblads, Rachel and Jeff, Amy and Elijah, the Wadsworths, the Schilkes, Kat Goltz, Lauren and Chris, Nathan Mayes, Frances and Andy, Karrie Dawley, Molly Watts, Bex Morton, the Axtmayers, the Lambs, Ivy and Sung, the Beans, Claire and Jason, Kent and Debby, Heather and Stephen, and the Yutzis. Words will never say thank you enough.

To Tamara, Julie, and Allison for being health practitioners who went above and beyond what was ever asked or expected of you: thank you.

Cover photo: Donavan Waldrop
Audio engineer: Sam Fisher
Editor and cover designer: Lauren Murphree

CHAPTER ONE

Valleys of Depth

"But I am like an olive tree
Flourishing in the house of God;
I trust in God's unfailing love forever and ever.
For what you have done I will always praise you
In the presence of your faithful people.
And I will hope in your name,
For your name is good."
Psalm 52: 8-9 (NIV)

IT'S INTERESTING HOW chronic illness can completely change your life. One minute you're laughing uncontrollably with a friend, and then somehow, out of nowhere, you are staring at the face of suffering. This kind of suffering is unpleasant, to say the least. Like a hurricane, it seems to wipe out what all you had before and maybe even took for granted. You think to yourself, "I did not sign up for this!" But suffering gets more comfortable as it sits in your lap, reminding you of how much astronomically harder your life

1

is now.

How do we get through the suffering? Do we muster up all our strength and pull ourselves up by our bootstraps to get through it? Do we hit our knees in prayer and surrender ourselves to the Lord? Do we pout? Do we freeze? Do we blame?

I've done all these things to get through my wilderness of suffering. This wilderness began when I was nine years old, the year I was diagnosed with a disease that drastically changed my quality of life. Now, 19 years later, it still affects me every day.

It has brought out the worst in me; it has brought out the best in me. The strength and the joy that God has given me through it has been undeniable. It has pushed me beyond my limit a billion times, and it has shaken me to my core. It is unbearable on my own.

Battling lyme disease has been a cruel and lonely journey that I don't wish upon anyone. Like many others who have dealt with lyme, I wanted to escape out of my body for many years. Ten years ago, when I started having a hard time sitting in chairs because of how much pain I was in, I never imagined being here today still experiencing pain as I sit and write. Still not seeing healing in the way that I thought I would.

This is not the end of my story, though. It is still being written. And this past decade has been full of twists and turns and moments I'll never forget, like riding down a slide with roller blades on, getting on countless planes, ferries, trains, and buses, and meeting people who would forever change my life.

This fire of affliction is not a hopeless place but rather a deep place. It has not come into my life without true hope, joy, peace, rest, beauty, connection, and purpose, who have all been sitting here around the fire with me. They've always been holding hands with me through the suffering.

Contradicting parts of my life have all slowly become intertwined. Grief and joy. Hope and despair. Pain and blessing. Depression and gratitude. Tears and comfort. Losses and provision beyond comprehension. Loneliness and community that has been like family.

This morning, as I sit in my backyard and stare at a Colorado winter wonderland doused in pine trees that are full of immaculate wonder, I sense the Lord saying, "here is a tiny visual glimpse into the work that I do in people only through their suffering." I imagined all the intricately designed snowflakes all coming together to form this pure, sort of crown that blankets everything that appeared dead on the ground to make it all look beautiful.

When I've had the eyes to see, God has unfolded some of His heart to me in the midst of pain. I don't think I would've seen those parts without all the suffering. Still, I don't fully know why God allowed an inhumane sort of suffering that has made my body feel broken for so many years. Why He delays healing when we know that He can - one of the many why's we all can internally ask when we experience anguish beyond repair.

Even though I can't fully understand, and the whys probably won't be answered til Heaven - that is, if I even care to know anymore once I'm there - to still breathe Him in and know that He is here is a gift. To feel chronic pain inside of my body and yet feel joy and peace instantaneously is a gift. To still have hope and belief that this isn't the end for me - it's all a gift from God. And in the between, in the waiting, I see miracles.

When I was nine years old, I didn't know that my entire life would be flipped upside down all because of a tick. I couldn't foresee my bubbly social self slowly becoming isolated or facing depression that threatened to take me down into its dark vortex, never to see daylight again. I didn't get a warning light or a letter in the mail notifying me that I would be fighting with every fiber in my being every day only to get results that felt like punishment with little to no relief, that I'd have to move on my own to other states and even another country for lyme disease treatment, or that my body would be forced to use a wheelchair at 26 years old.

What I also didn't know was that I'd have countless amounts of people of all walks of life praying alongside me, supporting me, reminding me who I was in God's eyes, and showing me glimpses of Jesus all along the way. I didn't know that God wanted to show me His love in the most intricate of ways, in ways that I don't see how would've been possible without the suffering.

I had no idea how much my life would be drenched in God's redemption and pure grace amidst pain. My life would be challenging beyond belief, but it'd also be rich, raw, and authentic. A life that when I'm old and gray, I'll be grateful to God that He entrusted me with, to know He could turn it into something good.

For years, "suffering" was not a word that I liked to use when describing my life. I thought it implied pity. But it doesn't. It's a massive part of my story and hundreds of millions of other people's stories too. We're in good company because it was also a huge part of Jesus' story as he walked this earth. He knows suffering. He doesn't run away from it, and he doesn't deny it even when it's a silent suffering. He makes Himself available to us for wisdom, guidance, comfort, and an abundance of other needs we have in our wildernesses.

If you're anything like me, you want more meaning in the suffering. You don't want to be consumed by the pain. You want your valley seasons to be valleys of depth. I don't mean depth like posting something vulnerable on Instagram that gets a bunch of likes, I mean depth in our relationship with the Lord; purpose, growth, and true meaning that comes from the Giver of life.

Dealing with an isolating disease has created a stronger desire in my heart for genuine relationships that go beneath the surface. These relationships tend to be the ones that last. They're the ones that are there for people through their tragedies. They're the ones that simply give people permission to be seen exactly as they are because when we're seen by one another for who we truly are, then we can love and be loved by one another authentically.

Being seen in our suffering is much harder to do than be seen when we're doing well because we are delicately vulnerable. Our lives look nothing like we envisioned them to, and it's scary to allow anyone into that space. We're tired of waiting, and so we shut ourselves in our bedrooms because we'd rather be seen when the suffering is over.

I'm wrestling between letting myself be seen in my suffering and being a recluse who's shut off from the rest of the world because it feels much easier that way sometimes. I want to wait to share my life with people until I'm completely healed, but I've come to see that we don't have to wait to share our testimonies until we're fully healed. We don't have to wait to live our lives until we're fully healed.

I still believe God is using my suffering. Even still, some of the trials I've walked through have made absolutely no sense and made me question everything. I've yearned for resolve, answers, and apologies that may never take place.

My heart is to bring you along on a journey towards wholeness that I'm still struggling to walk through as you read the pages to follow. I'm not offering another bible study or another diet that healed all my ailments or another form of treatment that I think everyone needs to try. What I have to offer are stories that I believe all point back to the Creator. Hoping that as you read these stories, you are encouraged and reminded of how faithful our God is.

My desire is not to over-spiritualize things, nor am I trying to create my own theology on suffering, healing, or spiritual warfare that's based on my own experience instead of God's word. My goal is to understand more of God's heart in suffering through His word and revelation.

We overcome by the blood of the lamb and the word of our testimony (Revelation 12:11). Part of me writing this book is to put the "overcoming with the word of my testimony" into practice. The enemy can't stand against our testimonies because they're undeniable proof of God's heart for hurting people in a hurting world.

More

You inevitably change when you are fighting for your life for so long. A myriad of worldly goals and desires begin to mean little to nothing to you. Time slows down, and life becomes rawer than before. The way you walk, the way you talk, the way you interact with your friends. You find joy and laughter for your own sanity.

Chronic illness affects every one of your relationships. Most of your friends and family wonder why you still can't do all the daily activities they're doing, and they're still baffled as to why you haven't been healed. They want a simple fix. You do too.

It affects your work. Your brain doesn't keep up like your friend's brains do, and you struggle to find grace from society to say it's okay to take another sick day when you look perfectly healthy. Your medical debt keeps piling up. You eat rigidly healthy for years and try to stay as active as you can, but it doesn't change how sick you feel all the time.

If you can relate to anything I'm saying, I am so sorry. Lyme disease that doesn't go away feels like an uphill trek with no definite answers or breaks from pain and exhaustion. It's a massive inconvenience to both my husband and me every day, but it's so much more than an "inconvenience." It has totally altered our lives.

Ironically, lyme has been an invaluable teacher in my life. It has forced me to practice patience, rest in God, forgive myself and others, live kindly, have more grace, grieve, and speak my needs. This journey has completely changed my mindset, the way I love, the way I worship, and the way I engage in life. And despite the scars, crushed dreams, and immeasurable losses, I've somehow been softened through it.

I've been hearing so much about being strong these days,

but I believe there are times that being weak and soft is right where we're supposed to be. Sometimes it's good to be soft like silly putty. When I bring my weaknesses to the light, God gives me His strength. When I soften and open my hands that are full of needs, God touches those needs. When I acknowledge to God what I am incapable of and ask Him to do whatever He wants to do through my shortcomings, He has a pliable life to work with, like a piece of clay in His hands.

Though I haven't always felt it, Jesus has been near to me in my suffering. Every. Single. Day. His presence and friendship with me have carried me through my darkest days. He has also seemed distant, silent, and cruel at times. Yet still, I look back on each year and I can see that the Lord has used an invisible disease in profound ways. He has used people all around the world that could've never been the hands and feet of Jesus to me if I never had chronic illness.

I've had remarkable health practitioners, friends, Christians, non-Christians, and even strangers bless me beyond belief along the way. Some fed me; some gave me clothes, some housed me, some worked hard to treat the disease in my body, and others gave me financial support for treatment. Some wrote me letters and cards, some visited me, some loved me in ways that can't ever be put into words. But they're all His instruments; make no mistake in hearing that it's all been Jesus. He wanted me to know that, and I think He wants you to know too. I wouldn't be sharing my story if I didn't believe that people needed to hear it. This healing, this surgery of my heart, mind, spirit, and soul that God has been performing since I was a little girl has left me more humbled, and I believe more understanding of His love than a life without pain.

You might be reading this and saying, "great, I'm so glad that you found purpose in your pain and that you were able to grow from it. I'm not there. I don't know if I'll ever be there." Friend, I just want to sit with you right now and tell you that it is okay. You're not called to spontaneously create a pretty picture out of a catastrophe. None of us are. Only God can do that. Today I came across the words of another lyme warrior, Alisa Turner, and I found her words refreshing. I hope you do too.

"To The One Suffering...

You do not need to suffer well. You don't have to find the joy. It's completely okay if you don't praise Him in the storm. He'll understand. You don't need to find a purpose for your pain. Or the beauty in the ugly of what you're going through. You don't have to look for the light or be the light amidst the darkest days of your life. You don't have to act ok if you're not ok. There is no additional expectation or pressure on you upon what is already crushing you to death.

God's mercies are new every morning but yet by sunrise you may be worse, declining, desperate more than you were the night before. Some of you are barely breathing, barely holding on. You might be prayed for and they will claim a miraculous healing, and still nothing changes. That is not on you. You may be dismissed, belittled, or entirely not believed. You may be abandoned or forgotten when the timeline of this crisis extends beyond people's capacity. You may never find the words to express the hell you walked. And even if you do, you may be too afraid to speak them.

And... At some point in this unimaginable journey, you may overcome, you may be medically or miraculously healed, you may find the Joy again, you may be a champion advocate, you may write a book, you may get to help others who are where you used to be. But those things are optional, not required of you for what you endured. YOU SURVIVED. And that is enough."

There may be no inspiration that you and I can pull out of thin air because sometimes we have pain so deep with no visible way out of it before Heaven, and sometimes there never is. We're left with unresolved problems and unanswered questions, and it seems impossible to find resolve or see God's heart in our circumstances anymore.

I think we still might long for more depth in our suffering, though. In my own complete brokenness of body and soul, I know I did. All my forms of self-help and self-improvement failed me, leaving me yearning for more. That "more" was Jesus, though many days I did not recognize it.

Though I fought it, deep down in my heart, I wanted more than to mediocrely get through the pain until it all went away. What if I learned from the One who didn't try to get out of the wilderness even though he was the son of God? What if I was refined like gold? What if Jesus changed my heart in the process? What if I didn't grow bitter or resentful towards the people who wronged me and falsely accused me? What if my heart was healed amid unfathomable suffering?

A Journey Toward Wholeness

Jesus can profoundly change our hearts at any moment. He brings radical transformation that can't be denied. Another life is set free, redeemed, healed, delivered. Sometimes it happens in a blink of an eye; other times, the transformation is gradual. It's fascinating to see someone who has come to know the Father's heart in such a way that they're hardly recognizable from the person they once used to be.

Jesus will inevitably glorify Himself through our lives when they're surrendered to Him. Believe it or not, He can and will use the even most devastating pain that we face. Even the parts of us that can feel ugly and completely broken.

True wholeness is found in Jesus. Sure, you can find cheap forms of love and healing out there, but they won't sustain. Jesus is the only one who can bring the kind of healing that our souls are longing for. He's the only one who can speak tender healing words over the wounds that nobody else knows about.

Deep down, every one of us yearn for this wholeness. Not only physically, but mentally, emotionally, and spiritually. We want to be balanced and we want to thrive. Not only for ourselves, but for our loved ones. We want to be able to keep showing up during our painful seasons, even when isolating sounds like the better option.

This kind of healing - this healing of the soul - confronts parts of ourselves that we don't want to face even though they are in desperate need of healing. When you're undergoing a surgery on your soul, it's long and it's multifaceted. It requires honesty and rawness. It's a deep work that has no end-all, be-all step-by-step manual or program that has the exact same results for everyone. There is no universal formula to becoming "whole," but God takes us all on individual journeys that are unique to the way He created us.

If you're reading this book, maybe it's because you've been diagnosed with lyme disease or another life-altering condition. A healing like this - a journey towards wholeness - is not for the faint of heart. It takes grit. It takes even more gentleness. It's a deep work that feels invisible much of the time.

What we want is to go to the doctor, take a pill, and be all better. But that's not how it always works with chronic illness, nor is that how it always works with the Lord. Sometimes you have to dig deep with the Lord, and sometimes you feel completely broken and undone for a season (or many seasons) before you start to truly heal and recover. Inner healing is a process.

I believe our minds, bodies, spirits, hearts, and souls are all greatly intertwined with one another. When one is hurting, it throws the others off-kilter. Many people I meet who have chronic illnesses have gone through very traumatic experiences. Those traumatic experiences have taken a toll on every part of them, and their bodies are having a hard time knowing how to cope anymore. Their limbic systems are not working correctly anymore.

Take a moment to look around at the world we live in. We weren't created to operate or eat the way that society has deemed what's normal or even "healthy," for that matter. We were given brains to think for ourselves, and we can discern when something isn't good for our bodies. We were made to thrive on what God has made for us to eat without all the pesticides, antibiotics, hormones, msg, GMO, and artificial flavors added - can I get an amen? We weren't made to be sitting in cubicles for eight hours a day or popping medication to get through our next meeting.

Maybe you're in the middle of processing through a scary diagnosis, and you don't know how to cope. Perhaps you're relearning your body and what it can and can't handle. Maybe you don't have a diagnosis to name the turmoil you're going through, and you don't know what to do anymore.

Maybe you have a child or a spouse or friend struggling with their mental health. Perhaps you're searching for God in your trial, and maybe you're not seeing Him. Maybe you're jaded. Maybe you're not getting the results from medical treatment that you were hoping for or seeing God's promises being fulfilled in your life the way you thought they would be.

Maybe you aren't physically sick, but you're sick of life in general. Many of us are right now. I want to remind you that your life matters. There's significance to your life, and you are valued more than you know. If you aren't well, it matters that you get proper treatment for your condition.

Hear me when I say this: you are worth it. I repeat: you are worth it! You're priceless, and your life is of great value. You are the light of the world (Matthew 5:14-16), and your body is a holy temple that was made to shine bright in this ever-increasing dark world.

It matters that you grieve the traumas and tragedies you've experienced. Your experience is something that nobody can take away from you. It all matters. Not a day in the story of your life has been unseen by God, whose love for you is never-ending.

A diagnosis is just that - a diagnosis. It doesn't define us. It doesn't have power over us. It's something that was spoken out loud by a doctor, but the word of the Lord is incomparably more powerful. So, why aren't we healed yet?

Even if we speak out His word daily and aren't healed, there's nothing wrong with us. It may not feel like it at all, but the truth is that He honors those who suffer day in and day out, and He can use our pain in the most unexpected moments. I assure you that He has a plan, and He's writing a unique story through your life. And even though He's written the most remarkable story of all time, God still values all our individual stories and brings purpose to them.

Your story matters. Here's mine. Here is a story about the radical love and faithfulness of God.

Disclaimer: I don't have the answers. I'm not a doctor or a bible scholar, and I still can't wrap my mind around some things that have happened in my life or the lives of some of my friends who have suffered in various ways. As I look around and see all the tragedies around me, the world feels dark. I know that many of us are struggling to see God's goodness or faithfulness as we stare at our unfortunate circumstances or the circumstances of others.

As I share about how good God has been to me in the midst of pain, some of you may be struggling to believe that there is a God. Some of you may be struggling even to see a point in living anymore. My only request is that you stick with me to the end of this book because I can tell you that there is a Holy, faithful God who is good beyond our belief. There is a reason for living - I can assure you of that.

Now as Jesus was passing by, He saw a man blind from birth, and His disciples asked Him, "Rabbi, who sinned, this man or his parents, that he was born blind?" Jesus answered, "Neither this man nor his parents sinned, but this happened so that the works of God might be displayed in him...." John 9:1-3 (ESV)

CHAPTER TWO
A Beast Named Lyme

I will rejoice and be glad in your steadfast love,
because you have seen my affliction;
you have known the distress of my soul,
and you have not delivered me into the hand of the
enemy; you have set my feet in a broad place."
Psalm 31: 7-8 (ESV)

Lyme disease. As I write those two words, you may have PTSD from reading them because you know the torment, the trauma, the exhaustion, and the downright hell that can come with those two words. Welcome to the world of borrelia, co-infections, parasites, mold, heavy metals, candida, mycoplasma, interstitial cystitis, lyme carditis, endometriosis, infertility, and the list goes on. If you're a loved one of someone with lyme disease that won't go away, you probably know a good amount about it too, and it has probably affected your life immensely as well.

Lyme can manifest itself in so many ways. Some have become paralyzed on one side of their face or bodies, some have lost their sanity, while others are entirely bedridden on feeding tubes or IV antibiotics 18-20 hours a day. Each chronic case typically has specific co-infections among other bacterias and complications to different degrees that make each person's symptoms unique.

I've been diagnosed with lyme, ehrlichia, bartonella, babesia, rickettsia, candida, endometriosis, lupus, diabetes, Epstein Barr virus more times than I can remember, one of the most dangerous parasites in the world that destroys your heart and is supposedly incurable, among other diagnoses along the way. Lyme and co-infections have typically manifested themselves in my body as peripheral neuropathy, unbearable neck and back pain, brain inflammation, loss of energy and consistent mobility, jaw pain, tremors, sharp pains all over my head and body, heart palpitations, organ pain, weakness and numbness in various parts of my body, cognitive dysfunction, arthritis, losing control of things in my hands, heat intolerability, memory loss, insomnia, chest pain, a feeling of bugs crawling under my skin, irregular breathing, ruptured ovarian cysts, endometriosis, panic attacks, fits of rage (lyme rage is a real thing), depression, anxiety, no appetite, nausea, sensitivity to sound and light, my heart rate skyrocketing when going from lying down to sitting or standing, feeling like my muscles are rocks, slowed motor skills, heart and lung weakness, muscle spasms, inability to do simple things at times like open jars, tinnitus, mood swings, intense adrenaline for no reason, feeling like my brain and body are vibrating, paresthesia, feeling like my body is on fire after 30 seconds of exercise, endless body aches, abnormal body temperature, and dizziness to name a few. Most of these symptoms have went on for the last decade – that is, until very recently.

I used to wake up feeling like the back of my head was on fire, my hands and feet numb, my brain feeling like it was shaking, my neck and back feeling broken, and all I wanted to do is break everything within sight. This is the reality for many people who have lyme. Strangely, knowing that I'm not the only one who has experienced this can be somewhat comforting. I'm not sharing the raw parts of my story for pity, I'm sharing it to speak up for the millions and millions of others who feel voiceless, depressed, misunderstood, among many other negative side effects and feelings that come with having lyme.

Every day I've been a student of suffering. Some mornings I've been belching out worship songs, and others, I've been lying in bed, not saying a word. Not wanting to move all day. To feel like your nervous system, spinal cord, and every system in your body is being hijacked every morning is something that's hard to put into words. I can give myself massive amounts of grace and self-love, but that does not sustain me. What I've learned is that I'm not in control of lyme, but I am in control of keeping my heart soft and receiving grace that only comes from God.

A couple of years ago, this is what I wrote in my journal: "It's 5 AM. I fell asleep with shooting pains in my hands, feet, and spine. I woke up early to sharp pains in my insides. Eating and sleeping have become a luxury. I have burning nerve pain. My joints ache more and more. My heart and organs feel weaker than they did yesterday. Going on day 3,285 [roughly] of chronic pain in my spine. It feels like someone is pushing on the left side of my skull. My jaw is killing me. There are more unexplainable health problems that I've never had before, and we have no idea why. My brain is moving so slow, and it's hard to control my hands and feet in the morning. It's hard to walk. I get up, go into the living room, and turn on the light. I open my bible. I cry. My husband, Andy, comes to sit with me. We are exhausted. We are fighting to believe. We are fighting with everything we've got."

There are still days that I feel trapped in my body. But now, I have the tools to work through those emotions. Because with chronic illness comes heavy emotions. The only One who can handle those emotions is God. Lyme would be impossible for me to cope with without God.

Odd forms of medical treatment have become a lifestyle for me. As I write this, I'm lying in a hyperbaric oxygen chamber because it can be tremendously helpful. I've stuck more tubes inside of me than I can ever count, tried every diet possible from entirely plant-based to being a carnivore to even eating nothing but beef literally for weeks on end (who wouldn't after hearing Mikhaila Peterson's success story with it?). I've had bee venom injected all over my spine, sat and laid in odd contraptions all over the country, flown across the world for medical help, and put my body in below negative 250 degrees Fahrenheit like it was a science project. You name something that promotes healing or kills lyme... I've probably tried it, all in an effort to get my life back.

From 2010 to 2018, it is estimated that nearly half a million Americans were diagnosed with lyme disease every year. That's 59% more than the estimate of 300,000 cases per year which was previously listed on CDC's website. That estimate does not include the countless number of misdiagnosed cases.

Experts in the medical and scientific community, as well as major legislators, have deemed lyme disease an epidemic and a national public health crisis. Lyme is one of America's fastest-growing infectious diseases and is yet the most misdiagnosed, inaccurately tested, and least funded. Even with the advances that they've made over the years, proper testing is pricey, and even then, the testing can be inaccurate.

Then there are the hundreds of thousands of people who still have lingering symptoms many years or decades after they got diagnosed. Most of those people went through promising expensive treatments that put them into more debt. Some of those treatments may have ended up making their health worse, making it impossible to keep up with medical bills or treatment, for that matter.

Chronic lyme isn't recognized as a real condition and lyme disease is still not being recognized properly - which is strange when too many lives to ever count around the world are being ruined by this disease, when people are losing decades and decades of their lives, when so many have lost their lives due to lyme. I don't care if you call it chronic, late stage, or whatever else you want to call it. Just don't say it's not real because it only reiterates to everyone who has it that you don't believe them.

Chronic illness can be so multifaceted. Sometimes I think it's the body's way of saying, "please slow down. Please let yourself grieve and mend the trauma you've endured." Other times it's simply a perfect storm whether that be from a toxic exposure such as mold, pesticides, or chemicals mixed with viruses or chronic inflammation that's already in someone's body due to high levels of stress or high EMF exposure and radiation like from smart meters. Sometimes, it doesn't have to do with emotional, physical, or mental trauma. But what I'm finding is that many people with chronic illness find more profound healing from past wounds that may have never been fully dealt with had they not gotten so sick and sensitive to our world.

When I was nine years old, I, including most people with lyme or knowing someone with lyme at the time, barely knew anything about it (besides, perhaps the few determined geniuses who looked like crazy people to the rest of the world). My parents and I didn't know how long it had already been in my system or what kind of effects it would have on me for the years to come. We didn't know all that came along with that diagnosis or how difficult attaining remission would be as an adult. We didn't know that specific genetics cause certain people to have a much harder time fighting off something as tricky as lyme. As many people have found, maybe including yourself, antibiotics don't always do the trick and help ease your symptoms or get you into remission, for that matter.

To be more accurate, the antibiotics "should" do the trick if you're diagnosed and treated for 30-45 days immediately after being infected, but they are less likely to if borrelia (lyme bacteria) has been in your system for a while. Most people I talk with who have lyme went through years of seeing doctors who knew nothing about it and were told something along the lines of, "you're just depressed" or "you're a hypochondriac."

Lyme is radically unpredictable. Something that could be healing to you one day could have the complete opposite effect on you the next day. Spending the last decade not knowing what the next day or moment was going to look like, whether I laid in bed all day or pushed my body too far - the inconsistency of it all - is a piece of the whole bargain that has always been incredibly hard for me to cope with. I've never gotten used to that.

The days that you feel legitimately "well" are very few and far between. Your "good days" are such a tease because tomorrow, you will likely barely be able to walk to the bathroom or take care of yourself. One minute you're riding a bike, and the next, you're on the couch for three days, barely able to do anything. You become more resilient than you ever thought was possible.

If you have lyme, I can guess that you probably don't feel like there's much of a place for you anymore. You may feel a bit forgotten. Like many with lyme, you may have disappeared entirely from society. You may not even want to live anymore.

You may have also felt stripped of your dignity for multiple and complex reasons. You've probably lost a lot of relationships. Many if not most times, when you've tried to commit to something, you haven't been able to follow through because of the never-ending pain and fatigue you experience. You may have lost a good deal of your confidence because you doubt yourself after countless times you haven't been able to show up for that friend or family member the way they need it; you haven't gotten a fair shot to be the employee you want to be.

If you're married, there's likely some trauma that you and your spouse have had to go through solely due to lyme.

There's probably been countless hard choices and sacrifices you've made together along the way because lyme has likely sucked you and your spouse's energy to keep up with everything.

Your spouse may also suffer from poor health, or maybe even lyme. Theirs may or may not be less severe than your case, or their health may be run down from the physical and emotional burden that comes along with watching you suffer every day, but either way: to watch the people you love gradually lose their quality of life as their health deteriorates is devastating. It reveals a little glimpse of how our spouses and loved ones feel toward us every day: helpless.

If you desire to have children, that's probably not a good idea until you're in complete remission since lyme could be passed through the embryo and other detrimental complications that can happen due to lyme affecting your ovaries and hormones. If you have children, you may have had lyme before you got pregnant, and now your kids may have been diagnosed with lyme as well. Lyme affects the whole family.

The empathy you typically receive upon being blatantly honest about how terrible you feel is somewhere along the lines of, "oh, I'm sorry you're not feeling well," with an uncomfortable linger in the air for the remainder of your conversation. Or they say something like, "oh yeah, my second cousin has 'lymes' disease."

You are left many nights in the quietness of your bedroom that is filled with painful memories, your mind racing with what you could do differently to change the next day - no matter how disgusting something tastes or how hard a treatment protocol is, or how awful the side effects are that you may experience. You desperately want a different outcome. You want your life back.

The Right Kind of Detour

Lyme has never been an easy thing for me to be open

about, but I have seen God do unbelievable things when I've been honest about it. Maybe it will help someone else know that they aren't alone. Maybe it will help bring awareness to lyme disease. Perhaps it will help others process their journeys. I hope it does, but I want more than that. I believe that sharing some of what I've gone through shows that God is still good even in the kinds of suffering that are hard to live through and gives more weight to His undeniable faithfulness that has taken place in my own suffering.

After doing a western blot test when I was nine years old, lyme had already done a lot of damage. I had severe arthritis in my joints like a little old lady. Many years later, I found an old journal of my mom's. She wrote that I couldn't walk from the dining room to the couch in the next room, so I would lie on the floor until I got the energy to get up again.

I don't remember much from that season or my childhood, for that matter. Still, I do remember that it was a process of getting healthy again after taking countless antibiotics for a long time, and my friends wondering why I had missed so much school or why I had random symptoms like my face being pale white or getting red and purple rashes from vigorously itching myself.

Lyme seemed pretty non-existent during most of my teen years, despite the numerous injuries, multiple cases of mono, periods that lasted nearly two weeks, procedures like getting my tonsils removed, joint aches, and immune-induced problems. As much as those things sound like red flags now, at the time, there was so much chaos going on for our whole family, occupying everyone's time and energy. Dad was out having affairs and drinking himself to death while mom was left picking up the pieces and taking care of us three kids.

When I was eleven, my family and I moved from Michigan to Tennessee. Six months later, my parents got divorced.

When I was 15, I was a passenger in a severe car accident that put a toll on my back. When I went to the ER, they checked me for a concussion. I never got my back checked out. I remember having to lay down because it was too painful to sit and being unable to participate in track practice - which was an enormous part of my life at the time.

A couple of years later, during my senior year, while training for the state track competition, I dead-lifted a bar over 100 pounds with my back instead of my legs. As I dropped the bar back onto the floor like a hot potato, my back cracked it in a way that it was not meant to, and I immediately felt pain. I got it checked out by a specialist and was told that some of the discs in my back were bulging inward. I was advised to never pursue running competitively again.

At 17 years old, my little world that I'd built on running my heart out and wearing my gold and silver track spikes came crashing down once I settled into the fact that I couldn't run in college even though I kept talking with college track coaches about scholarships because it's all I wanted at the time. Looking back, I see God's hand in my life.

I decided to take my first semester of college off to pursue missions, which had been on my heart ever since I was young. I signed into Skype and called up my uncle Rich who I had only met a couple times in my life. He and my aunt Debbie had started a YWAM (Youth with A Mission) base in Panama nearly 20 years prior and had been full-time missionaries there ever since.

I asked Rich if I could come volunteer for the summer, and in return, he suggested I come in the Fall for a two-month-long outreach backpacking through the tribes of Panama. So, I bought a flight and went.

The people I met during those two months touched my own heart much more than I probably ever touched theirs. It was there in those jungles that my heart softened, and I began to have a genuine relationship with Jesus. I became wrecked by the love of God and couldn't get enough of the way of life there, so I went back and did a discipleship training school (DTS).

I could probably write a book on that experience alone, but in short, it was one of the best experiences of my life. Jesus found me there and filled me with indescribable meaning and life. I wasn't the same girl who moved to Panama that summer as the one who graduated from my DTS alongside six young women who had become like sisters to me over the course of only five months.

As I found myself living on foreign soil, I was taken by the uniqueness of the Ngöbe-Buglé, Emberá-Wounaan, and Guna tribes. I was flabbergasted by how each person we stayed with made the best food they had in their possession and served it to my friends and me.

I won't forget the surreal sounds of the hot and humid green jungles full of animals I'd never seen before, like sloths and tarantulas, or the old men walking around with their tropical fruits in one hand and their machetes in the other. I was reminded of how little on earth I knew when I heard words that made no sense and then had to have a translator explain to me what the words meant. I was in a place that was so unfamiliar, yet it felt like home.

Back With a Vengeance

While living in Panama, I began to experience the effects of lyme in many new and vengeful ways. During one of our seven-hour hikes during a survival camp, if my body had a gas tank, it would've been running on E. Then I ran out of gas. People who were in much worse shape than me were completely dominating me. I sat in the mud that day, wondering why my body wasn't working and what in the world was happening.

Chronic pain more prominent on the left side of my body was the first symptom that developed. My new norm was so different from before, and my quality of life began to lessen as days and months went by.

After living out of the country on and off for two years, the pain I experienced reached an unbearable point. At the time, I was serving as a full-time missionary where I had felt God led me to, which was just outside of Tijuana, Mexico, in a place called San Antonio Del Mar. I had just walked through almost two years of another round of mysterious health issues, without it even crossing my mind that it was lyme again. One doctor in Mexico told me I had kidney stones; another at an ER said it was simply a pulled muscle. Things weren't adding up, and I was feeling worse by the day.

I was confident that God would carry me through my health battle but was also confused. *"God, I know you led me here, but why has everything gotten worse since I've been here, and why can't doctors help me?"* As I walked the streets of the red-light district in Tijuana and prayed for prostitutes and transvestites, my health worsened. During our prayer walks and a weekly homeless ministry, we walked into extremely dark areas and situations. I had no clue about the war that was taking place in the spiritual realm or how to combat it.

I didn't understand the authority that I had in Jesus or how my relationship with Him was tremendously more important than any ministry ever would be. I didn't know how wise it would've been to ask the Lord himself if He was leading me into the dark places I went.

I didn't realize that ignoring what my body was telling me was ignoring the very temple of God. I had such zeal, but I lacked so much wisdom, and I lacked true rest in God. I was looking to my leaders and those around me much of the time to get the temperature or on what I was supposed to do next, rather than solely listening to the voice of God.

After living in Mexico for five months, I knew something needed to change. One day, while lying in my bedroom filled with bunk beds where my foreign friends and I crashed at night, I researched my symptoms (rarely do I do this nowadays with how scary the internet can be when you look something medical up), and I came across a condition called endometriosis. After being on birth control multiple times to try to manage ovarian cysts (the ones that ruptured made me not want to have ovaries in the first place), everything that was said about endometriosis totally lined up with what I had been experiencing.

Just like that, I sensed these words from a still small voice in my spirit: "you have endometriosis and lyme. Go home and get treated for it." I believe the Holy Spirit was warning me that day. I wanted to help other people, but I didn't know how to take care of myself yet. I packed a few things and flew home, thinking I would return to Tijuana within only a month or two.

When I returned to the states is when I started experiencing unusually intense spiritual warfare and attacks on my life, even more than when I was on the "mission field". As I sought out medical help, instead of receiving the medical treatment that I needed, doctors said obscure things. I was blamed for my condition. One doctor that my mom and I encountered ridiculed me and said I was sick because of my "lifestyle." He was a Christian.

I was put on numerous narcotics, and an antidepressant called Zoloft. Two weeks later, I threw the Zoloft pills down the toilet because they did not help me. I wasn't depressed; I was in debilitating pain. I continued the narcotics for about a year because they took the edge off chronic pain. I wasn't dealing with the root issues, though, so I continued developing many more debilitating symptoms.

"It's in your head" was the message that I was getting from the people who I thought I could trust. After not healing from back injuries years prior, I met with a back surgeon searching for any relief available. I had multiple cortisone, epidural, and steroid shots, all of which made me break out in rash, hives, and/or bruising and did not help the pain. The back surgeon told me that I would eventually learn to live with the pain. But lyme pain is a different kind of pain, and because it attacks the weak parts of your body, you can be left feeling crippled wherever your unhealed injuries are.

I remember one appointment with a pain management doctor who I was seeing for the first time. He told me that he was doing some sort of "scan" of my back. As I laid there on that table, to my surprise, the doctor suddenly injected my lower back with a steroid which I had literally just told him that I was allergic to and was not going to try any more of. That particular injection caused the nerves in my back to feel like they were hijacked.

My life felt like a nightmare that I would surely wake up from tomorrow. Many memories had been suppressed in our family due to trauma, including memories of me battling a severe case of lyme disease. I was left trying to prove something that had clearly happened as a child and was still happening.

When I told my mom and stepdad that I thought it was lyme disease, they brushed it off and told me it wasn't lyme disease. They said they didn't even know if I ever had it for sure. But I had it severely as a child, along with my dad, who was also diagnosed with lyme.

The shame I carried over my condition slowly began to multiply. I didn't understand what was happening in the spiritual realm, or how I needed to set boundaries. As I continued to hear lies, it was as if this dialogue in my head began saying something along the lines of, "well, maybe this is all in my head. Maybe this is all my fault."

I've wanted to have a simple explanation as to why my case has been so severe, but lyme doesn't play by the rules nor does it make much sense. Hindsight is always 20-20. Years of going untreated, childhood trauma, exposure to toxins, poor methylation (the MTHFR gene), heavy metals, living in moldy homes, and poor living conditions have all surely been contributing factors. No general doctor was going to know that, though, and had no way to perform specific kinds of testing to help me get to the root of the problem.

John 6:63 says, "It is the Spirit who gives life; the flesh is no help at all. The words that I have spoken to you are spirit and life" (ESV version). I had to learn how to rely on the Holy Spirit in order to sustain. I had to learn to let go of the spirit of offense. I also had to learn that sometimes you must fight for your health, and that's not something to feel guilty about. Guilt is not from the Lord. I didn't know that back then though; I believed lies about myself. Most days, I believed that I was a burden and that my condition was my fault.

Now, I know that I am a blessing. I know that I am a daughter of the King - my loving Dad, who sees me. I know that I am seated in Heavenly places and don't have to do anything to earn God's love. I know that God has given me gifts to be used. My limitations don't define me; I'm defined by what Jesus says about me, and I flourish because He is holding my hand.

There's still such a deep desire in my heart for complete healing in this lifetime. There's still a desire for more compassion from the body of Christ as I wait for that healing. But how do you explain needing support for something so difficult to explain: a disease that's been highly controversial that some people say is made up; a condition that is denied little to no aid by every insurance company you've ever known of?

I can't tell you how many times over the last decade I've been ridiculed. I can't tell you how deeply all the smart remarks have propelled me to hide my disease from people in order to guard myself against further hurt.

Experience taught me to have a smile on my face, especially any time I was at church. To be strong. To be an example for others. If I showed what was really going on, I typically felt judged or misunderstood. So, I shoved and suppressed the trauma that my body and heart were going through week in and week out for ten years. And it was exhausting.

While being chronically sick comes with its own pain and restraints, being misunderstood adds another thick layer to the whole catastrophe that can flat out shut you down. You can't eat the same food or sometimes even stay in the same home as your loved ones because Bluetooth, mold, gluten (along with every other inflammatory food), and many other random things have the potential to give you unbearable flairs that make you wish you never left your house in the first place.

The problem is that it feels nearly impossible to continually communicate well when you're sick for so long and finding people who have compassion for an invisible illness is extremely rare. The words you want to say in a gentler tone pile up, and you can't even remember half of what happened yesterday. If you're anything like me, all this chaos eventually caused you to shut down more and rarely open up to people about it anymore.

When I was 21, nearly two years of being chronically ill had passed before I was able to see an actual lyme specialist. That doctor did IGeneX testing, which showed that lyme was, in fact, one of the issues. I also finally got my first laparoscopy which showed that I also did have endometriosis, just as I had felt the Lord tell me years prior. All the growths causing immense pain were ironically only on my left ovary, which was on the same side of my body that had more pain and symptoms.

As many would say, it's never just lyme. Like an onion, lyme has layers. When I started seeing a standard lyme doctor, I didn't know that, nor was I getting any relief. The pain got worse by their protocols, medication, and other treatment methods.

If you have lyme, you may have gotten a lot worse before you got any better. You've probably gotten accustomed to herxheimer, or "die off" reactions, treating the disease from every angle and lightening your toxic load layer by layer. It can seem like an endless maze trying to figure out the right plan of action.

As I continued trying different forms of treatment and putting more antibiotics in my system, I began to put countless hours into research and educating myself on the mysterious disease. I discovered more natural forms of treatment that were much more effective and better for my body and overall health. I realized that the health I was searching for would not be instantaneous but a process. I was seeking wholeness, not a band-aid over root issues.

If you've known me at all over the last decade, you probably haven't heard most of what I've just shared come out of my mouth before. I probably haven't told you what my body goes through daily or how much the disease has taken a toll on my life. Chronic pain is about as far as I typically go when explaining what it's like to people other than my husband or a very close friend. These symptoms, details, and stories aren't something that I carry around for people to see or know because I don't want to be defined by my pain and limitations.

Lyme is not what I want to focus on, nor has it been in the past. I've typically veered away from support groups or just sitting around talking about it for hours. I want to do something about it. I'm learning, though, that most good things take time and that being honest about what you've gone through is a part of the healing process and can help others know that they aren't alone.

Grace Over Guilt

Hundreds of millions of people have a similar story to this. The medical system failed them, and they didn't know where to turn for help. They went into medical debt because they didn't know how else to survive. They ended up isolated, debilitated, and confused.

If you've been diagnosed with lyme or another life-altering condition and haven't yet received the healing you've been praying for, I just want you to take a moment to honor yourself for coming this far. Maybe even give yourself a hug. You are strong. There's an indescribable strength that comes with battling chronic diseases and ailments that don't go away.

Allow yourself to soak in this truth: God has seen it all. Jesus has been at the right hand of God, interceding for you. The Holy Spirit has been illuminating your darkness. The Trinity is on your side.

"Therefore, he is able to save completely those who come to God through him, because he always lives to intercede for them" - Hebrews 7:25 (NIV)

Attention all weary souls who are bearing the burden of chronic illness: you are not alone. There is a whole community of silent sufferers out there. Then there is the greatest silent sufferer ever known to mankind. His name is Jesus.

He knew sorrow. He knew pain and loneliness. He knew ridicule. He knew being tempted and lied to by the enemy. He knew death and separation from the Father. And after all of that, now he lives to intercede for you. Those truths give me hope.

There's more to you and me than what we've been diagnosed with. That doesn't mean that what we're going through isn't real, and we can't just put a Jesus sticker over the grueling pain of our lives, and everything magically gets better. Some days we aren't okay, and we're not supposed to push through it in order to be okay. For some of us, the reality that we face in our bodies or minds can keep us locked up in our rooms, feeling isolated and empty.

I've lived in a great deal of denial and chronic guilt about my situation around just about everyone I know at some point. I've felt like an enormous burden. Maybe you have too. Or perhaps you've internally beat yourself up for not doing more. I've been there too, most days.

I don't see myself as a "lymie," nor am I a victim to what has happened to me. I detach myself from the disease. I see myself well and whole. I fully believe there's complete healing for me here on earth that has already been taking place for years.

Even after knowing God's truths and experiencing a deep fellowship with Him, having a long-term illness is still traumatizing, exhausting, and highly unpleasant. It is humiliating to ask for help when you don't look sick. It gets old to most people.

I think many of us with mysterious ailments and illnesses that don't go away feel downright guilty for not contributing to the world in the way we want to, which leads to feeling stuck. I've gotten stuck many days because I can't lower my standards for myself, or I compare myself with perfectly healthy people because I act and look just like them. These comparisons lead me into a big messy web of self-condemnation and guilt.

Guilt can become an endless cycle. I know because I've been in that cycle too many times to count. Sometimes the guilt can become bigger than the actual issue. That's what the enemy wants. He wants us locked up and unable to experience freedom.

God has continually invited me to know more of His tender grace in exchange for guilt. As His grace has poured over my wounds, layers of guilt have shed off my back. It's funny, right about when I think I've had enough grace and I need to pull myself back up by my bootstraps is typically when God's doing another work of grace in my life.

Sometimes His grace comes in the form of simply accepting help from people He puts in my life. Sometimes I have to reach out for His grace. Sometimes I have to ask for help even though everything inside me doesn't want to.

Swallowing your pride and asking for help isn't always easy. Wallowing in self-pity and thinking you're the victim all day can seem like the easier option. But that mentality doesn't get you very far in life.

Some days it may be too hard to do anything other than barely lift your head from the pillow. Some days you might be feeling like a victim. You may not have the courage to reach out to people, and that's okay. Just don't stop reaching out to God.

Amanda Cook has a song called Evergreen. This song has been so refreshing to me in my journey with lyme. In the song, she says, "there's no key I need to turn, there's no trick I need to learn, there's no mark I need to meet, Your love is evergreen. There's no war I have to fight, there's no need to be polite, there's no way I have to be; Your love is evergreen. There's no hill I need to climb, there's no flag I need to fly, there's no song I have to sing, Your love is evergreen."

There's immense freedom in Amanda's words. God isn't waiting for us to do something perfectly, nor is He withholding healing so that we pull ourselves together more. It's freeing knowing that it isn't on our shoulders to try to figure everything out or even do the "Christian" thing to do sometimes. It isn't about us; it's about receiving God's grace and living from that place. "Now the Lord is the Spirit, and where the Spirit of the Lord is, there is freedom" -2nd Corinthians 3:17 (NIV).

A Different Lens

Chronic illness has prohibited millions of people from their dreams, goals, desires, communities, and lives. It can be infuriating to watch people suffer in such an inhumane way and have no answers as they continue to fight for a proper diagnosis and proper treatment.

As many people have come to see firsthand over the last year or two, our medical system is corrupt. Our world is corrupt. Satan's still sneakily maneuvering his way like a puppeteer into people's minds and hearts just like he has for thousands of years. Darkness only looks like it's getting darker.

Amidst all the madness happening in our world and how much anxiety is bombarding our news feeds, there's a different lens that we as followers of Jesus get to have. It views circumstances with a unique perspective. When you look through the lens, you know that God can work all things out for your good and His glory. "And we know that

31

in all things God works for the good of those who love him, who have been called according to his purpose - Rom. 8:28 NIV). You know that the testing of your faith produces perseverance (James 1:3). The next verse in James 1 says, "let perseverance finish its work so that you may be mature and complete, not lacking anything." You know God's using suffering to refine your character.

You see the earth, all its fascinating history, you imagine the people who have walked the same ground that you are walking on thousands of years later, and you're reminded of the fragility of life. You see your body, a magnificent masterpiece, and you know that it's just a temporary tent for your soul to live in. Our earthly bodies will all eventually die, just like every other human body who has ever lived on earth. But you know that death is just the beginning. Earth is our temporary home.

When we look through these lenses, we value things drastically differently. We see God more clearly and desire to be closer to Him. We see who we are more clearly and love better because of it.

The lens reveals more of God's heart, gushing with an overflow of love for His people, even when everything appears dark. Beware because when you get more glimpses of His unstoppable love, you will change. Your heart will be transformed in the most unorthodox of ways. You will shed off your religion. When you truly get more in touch with the reality of His love, it will turn your world upside down.

Many days, like today, I have a hard time wearing those lenses. I know all those truths, but sometimes I want something more tangible.

What if years of yearning led us to being exactly where we need to be? What if God's using people who suffer to remind the church that God never leaves us even in the worst of circumstances? What if He's still using people's ailments to bring Him glory? What if He's waking up the church through pain, death, corruption, affliction, destruction, lies - all of which come from the father of lies?

What if God wants to show us more of His tender grace and strength through all our frailties and all that is happening in the world around us?

God is an all-consuming fire who can do exceedingly and abundantly more than what we can ask or think (Eph 3:20), and yet I somehow can still forget that truth in the moments when I'm not connected to Him. The truth is that He is the ultimate Physician. His power is incomparable to any doctor's tools. He's so much greater we can fathom.

He relates in ways nobody else can. He can handle every single one of our hurts and frustrations and is the only one who can bring the healing balm that we are in desperate need of. He is Jehovah Jireh, our provider. He is victorious over pain and disease. He has the final say.

I forget where I first heard this line, but it has stuck with me: "don't mistake a single defeat with the final defeat." When Jesus rose again, He defeated it all. He gave us salvation. He gave us a promise that our suffering would not last forever. He gave us eternal life.

He humbled himself, even to the point of separation from His Father, and after that He died on a cross declaring over all the anguish of life, he said, "IT IS FINISHED." He gave us the grandest gift of all time, the greatest redemption of all time, the deepest grace... and yet as if that wasn't enough, he gave us the greatest parting gift. Our friend and our counselor, the Holy Spirit.

"But the Comforter, which is the Holy Ghost, whom the Father will send in my name, he shall teach you all things, and bring all things to your remembrance, whatsoever I have said unto you. Peace I leave with you, my peace I give unto you: not as the world giveth, give I unto you. Let not your heart be troubled, neither let it be afraid."
-John 14:26 - 27 (KJV)

The immaculate parting gift that God left us as Jesus ascended back to Heaven. Do we realize how amazing this reality is? When Jesus left earth, God left us another form of Himself. That form is so holy, so beautiful, and has a way of illuminating our darkest days. What a priceless gift the Holy Spirit is to you and me in our battles.

Trusting the Holy Spirit's leading has personally been enormous in confronting lyme, reaching new levels of health, and sustaining every moment over the last decade. What the Spirit of God leads me to do every day may not seem monumental in the moment, but day by day the Spirit is continually leading me into more life, vitality, and wholeness. When the world is telling me to go right but there's a still small voice saying to go another way, I stop and listen. When I don't know what I should do, there in the quiet mundane moments, there's the Holy Spirit, gently guiding, gently assuring, gently pouring out peace.

This route is not necessarily the easiest by any means. Sometimes the route that the Holy Spirit leads me on is harder, but I can't judge whether I did the right thing based on the outcome. God knows the end of the story, and I trust He's leading me in the right direction.

I eventually flew back to Mexico to gather my belongings and say goodbye to my friends there. I spent four days back in the place where I believed the Lord had called me, feeling confused. Things weren't the same. People had changed, and so had I.

One thing I knew that God was telling me was, "I have something better for you." My last night there, alone on my knees in a dark room with the door locked and blinds closed, I wept. I told God that I didn't understand. I had come to this place because I thought it was where He was leading me, and yet He was pulling me away.

Kneeling on a tile floor, having no clue what my future held, I knew at that moment that God was there weeping with me. Now, nearly a decade later, I can still remember that evening crystal clear. It was one of the first times where I knew without a shadow of a doubt that Jesus was there with me. The inviting, safe sense of belonging there in the presence and sweetness of gentle Jesus. *Home.* Now, years later, I see things that God protected me from, and I am grateful. I see now how much God had to, and still is changing my heart.

A Fight for Freedom

Many people who have lyme are some of the strongest, most resilient people you'll ever meet. Most of them are judged and misunderstood on such a deep level and yet that doesn't stop them. From fighting all odds to beat their disease. From choosing to be grateful even though every day feels like a nightmare. From not letting their illness define them. From putting themselves out there again, knowing there is a potential of getting hurt. They keep pressing through to find root causes and solutions to their health problems.

The more I open myself up to know the lyme community, the more I see that these people are world changers. Lyme has given so many people a whole new and greater purpose in life than before they got sick. They are now the ones who are offering valuable tools and knowledge to help people who are in the same shoes they were once in. I see so many people still battling lyme going through various trainings and schools to educate themselves more because they truly want to help people. It is so inspiring.

I wonder what it will be like to look back on this time in history 50 years from now. I wonder what the medical system will look like. I wonder if it will have changed for the better.

Lyme is a beast. I think that there are many beasts we may encounter in our lives, chronic illness is only one. The beast could look like pride, fear, lust, worry, lies that we believe about God or ourselves, broken filters, greed, among other things that can all create barriers with God and those around us and keep us in a cage. So, how do we conquer these beasts?

For starters, we must know that there is an invisible battle going on for our souls every day - whether we are sick in our bodies or not. There's a battle going on for our minds. There's a battle going on for our hearts, our affection, and our attention. We need healthy spiritual awareness.

I've been one to typically brush off spiritual warfare messages in the past, or people who accentuate satan and all his tactics. I thought that if I paid no attention to the enemy and his demonic entities, it would all just be nonexistent. Why would I need to fight a battle that was already won?

What I was missing, though, were all those stories of Jesus giving us a model of what it legitimately looks like to be one of His disciples, which comes with a fair share of opposition and attacks. I forgot about those stories of Jesus completely going against the "norm" in the religious communities, dying to his flesh, driving out demons, being tempted by the devil even though He was without sin, and experiencing more righteous anger and going through more unjust suffering than any human ever has.

How did Jesus respond in those moments? He said, "do not put the Lord your God to the test" (Matthew 4:7). He said, "Worship the Lord your God and serve Him only" (Luke 4:8). He didn't engage with satan, He just spoke the word of God because he knew that satan can't stand against it.

"Then Jesus was led by the Spirit into the wilderness to be tempted by the devil. After fasting forty days and forty nights, he was hungry. The tempter came to him and said, "If you are the Son of God, tell these stones to become bread." Jesus answered, "It is written: man shall not live on bread alone, but on every word that comes from the mouth of God." -Matthew 4: 1-4 (NIV)

Since God has opened my eyes in new ways, I've been humbled by how naive of a Christian I used to be. Many times, our first blind spot is that we think that our battle is against people instead of satan. We start thinking people are the problem which only creates more division. For instance, we may believe that the enemy is a politician, the church, our parents, or worse: our spouse. We forget that "our struggle is not against flesh and blood, but against the rulers, against the authorities, against the powers of this dark world and against the spiritual forces of evil in the heavenly realms" (Ephesians 6:12 NIV).

If we are being attacked in our bodies or minds or any other part connected to us, we are not left defenseless trying to fight against those attacks. God is fighting for us whether we see it or not.

> So he said to me, "This is the word of the Lord to Zerubbabel: 'Not by might nor by power, but by my Spirit,' says the Lord Almighty" - Zechariah 4:6 (NIV)

We don't have to fight in our strength - if we do, we will fall apart. We rely on the Spirit.

Even in the challenges we face that can feel beyond bearable, we're still responsible for the posture of our hearts. So, how do you and I respond when we're in the middle of our own wilderness, when we're stripped of our comforts, and when we can't see a glimmer of hope in sight? Bitterness is not the answer. There is a better way to endure chronic disease than getting bitter towards the medical system or the people who have wronged us.

In our walks with Christ, there are only two ways you can go: closer to Him or further away. Better or bitter. Engulfed in more freedom or still enslaved in some areas. Our circumstances will undoubtedly change throughout life, and the choices we make aren't meant to be made through the lens of those circumstances but through the revelation of Jesus.

I believe there's a life of abundance awaiting you and I, and the pain we face can't ever take that away from us. It doesn't matter where we come from or what our limitations are; God doesn't want us cooped up with nothing or no one to help us. He intends to drench us with His love. He wants us in community. And even if we feel forgotten, God is still here with you and I, desiring better lives for us. He doesn't want us to be sick, but He may be allowing it for reasons beyond what we can understand.

The beasts may fight for our attention, but they will not win. One day, as we stare at our Father's glorious beaming face, all these momentary afflictions will become dust, and we will be free - fully free.

CHAPTER THREE

Rollicking in Canada

"For you, God, tested us;
You refined us like silver.
You brought us into prison and laid burdens on our
backs. You let people ride over our heads;
We went through fire and water, but you brought us to
a place of abundance"
Psalms 66:10-12 (NIV)

Now that I've shared with you some of the realities and struggles that come with living with lyme, I want to share some hope with you. I want to tell you some of the gifts I've found in suffering. I believe that I have been given priceless gifts, but all those things have only been merely acts of God. Only God has brought any good from my battle with lyme disease. So, here are some stories. These stories are proof of God's faithfulness and kindness amid suffering.

While living in Panama, I met a cool Canadian girl named Amy. We remained friends when I moved out to Mexico and when Amy moved back to Guatemala, where she had been before Panama. We both eventually ended up back in our hometowns – mine outside of Nashville, Tennessee, and Amy's outside of Ontario, Canada. Leaving Latin America was a hard adjustment for both of us. As we went through our own heartbreaks and other difficulties of life, I think God used our friendship to bring compassion to things in our hearts that some of the people closest to us couldn't understand at the time.

Fast forward to a couple of years later, at the beginning of 2015, Amy came to visit me in Tennessee on her way back up from visiting another one of our friends in Costa Rica. After departing Tennessee and returning to her home near Ontario, Canada - unbeknownst to me - Amy decided to buy a ticket for me to fly to her home in eastern Canada. When she called me to tell me what she'd done and said that she wanted to open her home to me as long as I needed to stay, I was dumbfounded. Her extravagant generosity caught me off guard. Not only was she opening her heart and her resources to me, her church and family all wanted to help me too.

My next step was obvious and simple: all I had to do was get on the plane. Honestly, though, it felt astronomical for me to follow through with that one simple step. I was following where the Lord was clearly leading, but I was going against what I was told I was supposed to do.

It was clearly a time for a fresh start. Yet, years of pain and shame told me to stay there in Tennessee. The reality, though, was that I had grown secluded there. I had lost my sense of meaning and purpose and was too sick to know how to move forward anymore.

In the early morning brisk hours on one fine day in May, Amy and I left the Syracuse airport, drove across the Canadian border, and into the charming and quaint town of Perth. After meeting many friendly people, Perth slowly became my safe place. The months that followed were filled with moments where I was learning to permit myself to fully let go and rest in order to heal.

40

I lived in bed most days, and many days it was a struggle to walk to the bathroom. Sometimes it was difficult to merely walk in a straight line without running into the wall or veering to the right because of equilibrium problems, and on a few occasions, I woke up with blurry vision. My friend was there watching, praying for me, fighting for me.

Amy gave up her space, her privacy, and the comfort of being in her cozy home alone so that I could have a place to start mending. A few years before inviting me to live with her, Amy had watched her own "Opa" ("grandpa" in Dutch) suffer immensely and eventually pass away. Instead of allowing that to turn away from others who were suffering, I believe she allowed the circumstances in her life to propel her to turn to the needy and tend to them *more*.

What Amy didn't know was that by letting me come stay in her cute little bohemian home with her for the summer - it changed me. It changed me before I even got on that plane and left Tennessee. She reminded me that people could be so loving and caring even when it's hard, uncomfortable, or easier to say no to instead.

I'll never forget the beautiful people from that community who rallied around me during that season and became like family to me. Their hearts to continually pray for me touched my own heart and humbled me. Healing was happening, just not in a place that I was expecting: in my heart.

Someone else who impacted my life during my time in Perth was Elijah. The friendly, goofy, sometimes timid, barefoot dude who wore a backward cap and carried a bible. Elijah was a light to his family and his community. Over the duration of my three months in Perth, he was frequently at the side of the bed praying over me.

I saw such passion in a brother who was growing in the Lord right before our eyes as he served and as he prayed over people on the streets. Tears flowed down my cheeks as Elijah prayed for me to be able to surf, run, and simply sit in a chair again because I knew the prayers came out of a pure, genuine place in his heart. He was one of the persistent widows, continually seeking justice and knocking on Heaven's door, asking God to heal me.

Another person in Perth that I'll never forget was Debbie. Debbie is paralyzed from the waist down, but that's not who she is. She is a kind and tenderhearted woman. Her heart is filled with love, and she doesn't live like a victim. One day while Debbie and I ate a meal together in her bed, I saw a spark in her eye in the middle of all her hardships. The kind of spark you know only comes from sitting with Jesus.

Debbie's husband, Bob, brings her food, helps her dress, and helps her in and out of the car. Bob is not just a husband but a full-time caregiver. We all have pain. Some pain is visible; some is not. Some pain is embedded into our hearts so deep underneath the parts we feel safe enough to share with anyone. Pain isn't meant to be compared. Sometimes the pain of the caregiver is equal or even more than the one being cared for. That pain may not be physical, but may be emotional or mental.

My time in Perth was a time of healing not only my heart but my soul. It was a kind of healing that seeped into the places in me that needed love from my family in Christ. The men of that community loved me well as their sister in Christ. That church family certainly bore my burdens, often reminding me of Paul in the bible. A sweet, older chap at the church said that he prayed for over 400 people every morning. They challenged me to invest in people and pray for them.

Friendship and community are extraordinary gifts to be gained in any season of life. When I think back on that time there with those friends, I am filled with gratitude. The Perth community challenged my faith, and their love and support for me inevitably changed my heart.

By the way, Elijah and Amy are now happily married with two adorable kiddos.

Our Adventure

"Trust in him at all times, you people; pour out your hearts to him, for God is our refuge" - Psalm 62:8 (NIV)

After living in Perth for a little over three months, God surprised me. I was in the middle of fundraising to go to a lyme institute in Florida, where I was planning on receiving specific treatments that had supposedly been the miracle cure for other lyme patients. I saw videos on their website of lyme patients in wheelchairs now walking and improving drastically. Though this seemed promising, every time I called to go over everything or order blood work from them, they kept upping their prices on me. What they said was originally going to be $8,000 was now $70,000. I couldn't keep up.

On a random whim, I called the founder and president of the Canadian Lyme disease association, Jim Wilson. I found his number online, and, to my surprise, he answered. He asked me to explain a bit of my story, and afterward, he said, "Lauren, there are only two doctors I would recommend to you at this point. Dr. Eric Chan and Dr. Julie Moore, and they're both in Vancouver."

My pastor at the time, Dan, was a blessing to me. Dan, his wife Amy, and their nine kids felt like family. Dan had coincidentally just shown me a video in his dining room of Dr. Chan out of all doctors in the world. I also knew someone in Perth with lyme whose symptoms went dormant on Dr. Chan's protocol. I immediately called both clinics. Dr. Chan said he could get me in on Friday, and Dr. Moore said she could get me in on Saturday.

Chan and Moore were over ten times cheaper than where I was initially going to get treatment. As if the stars didn't align enough, some special people gave me a generous amount of financial support to take care of my appointments, and whatever treatment entailed. I had been fundraising for months to go to a specific institute, all the while God had something better beyond comparison in store for me: an adventure.

I found a cheap flight going from the east side of Canada to the west; Dan said he would gladly pay for my ticket to Vancouver, and the rest was history.

Well, almost. I was initially going to stay with a pastor and his wife, whom pastor Dan knew from Vancouver. A few days before I left Perth, they told Dan something along the lines of, "we can't help her, our church can't help her, and she probably shouldn't even bother coming to Vancouver". I don't blame them, though; the couple knew little about me or my situation.

Then God told me that He had something better for me. Right before flying to Vancouver, my friend Roxanne said that she had a long-time friend named Aaron in Vancouver who was willing to let me stay with him.

It was scary going across Canada in the shape I was in where I knew not a single person, but I can still remember the joy I had knowing deep inside my heart that Jesus was with me, and He was holding my hand as I walked the departure runway towards the plane. His presence cast out any fear that lingered. Strength and joy filled my whole being as I sensed Jesus say, *"This is our adventure."*

It didn't seem like the time for an adventure. On the contrary, it seemed like a time to worry and lay in bed hopelessly every day until life got easier. But looking back, an adventure was exactly what my soul needed.

I was still a bit nervous, not knowing the guy that my friend had connected me with, but as soon as I saw Aaron standing there at the Vancouver airport holding up a sign, I knew that everything would be okay. Aaron is a goofy, easy-going, Jesus-loving fella who graciously opened his home to me - a modern apartment high above other buildings overlooking the city and majestic mountains. He was kind and stayed in his living room while I slept in the privacy of his bedroom.

After starting IV nutritional therapy and other forms of

treatment for the first time and giving my body what it had been depleted in for years, I began experiencing the best kind of change in my body that I had ever known. My treatments were going phenomenal, and for the first time, I was getting positive results instead of worse pain like I'd experienced in the past.

Within a week of treatment, I went from being debilitated to riding a bike for the first time in years. I went from having no idea where I was going to live to living in my favorite city I'd ever been to. I went from having no money to being provided for in ways that blew my mind, and my favorite part: I was feeling more like myself than I had ever felt before.

A couple of days later, a woman by the name of Belinda messaged me on Facebook and invited me to have dinner at her house. We didn't know each other, and neither of us remembers meeting the lady who connected us in Kingston, Ontario (who I eventually became friends with too). As my taxi stopped there in front of that house, I knew that it was no ordinary place. It was a charming three-story pink house tucked away on East Pender Street, one block away from East Hastings. East Hastings Street was dressed in syringes, old nonvacant run-down buildings, and homeless people laying all over its sidewalks. As you can imagine, the house stood out.

Though it may sound cliché, when I walked through that pink door, I immediately felt at home. The presence of Jesus was in that place. I met Adria and Belinda, two of the five kind souls who lived in the pink house. We had a lovely evening together as I laid on their couch like a vegetable and ate the scrumptious meal they had prepared. After staying with Aaron for a few weeks, the girls invited me to go on a camping trip with them.

At the end of the camping escapade, the girls asked if I wanted to come live with them. They had a spare hospitality room where they allowed underprivileged women who were in need of a place to stay free of charge. Without skipping a beat, I took up their offer and moved in.

The pink house changed my life. Not the house, but the people in it and the way of things in that place. From the way the morning sun came beaming into the hallway quietly ushering inspiration into your heart, to the faint, innocent giggles in the kitchen, to the warmth of hearing friends' worship in their bedrooms - it was all unusually sincere and real, which is rare to find in this world.

Christie is a humble, funny, gentle soul who is clearly committed to God and who loves those around her well. I look up to Christie in the way she lives her life and loves her community. She makes time to serve and love those around her, and she seems to find contentment and joy even in the hardest of times. Christie chose the call of God on her life and committed herself to serve the hurting people of east Vancouver. Many of these people are drug addicts, mentally ill, and oppressed. I'll never forget Christie playing delicate and lovely worshipful tunes on the piano. Those tunes were healing to my ears.

Adria is raw, generous, and kind. She's carefree about things that don't matter. One thing she said to me that's always stuck with me was "character always over career." She is hard-working but also doesn't get stressed over petty things. She doesn't care if people know how hard she works; she does the work unto God. She has genuine empathy for people; I saw it in her as she walked the streets and as she sat in the living room with the girls. Her purity of heart only becomes more real and evident the more you get to know her, and she is beautiful.

Arely is uniquely, gracefully, powerfully, Arely. God has used her to spout out His love all over the people she has worked with and served. She has astonishing stories from her life in the ways God has boldly used her, and it is evident that she walks with Jesus. Arely fights for the widow and the orphan, and she loves the "least of these."

Rachel is a sweet soul who loves with all her heart. She rejoices with those who rejoice and mourns when her friends fall away from The Lord. She showed me through her life examples of the story of the prodigal son and how the father runs to him and embraces him. It doesn't matter what the son has done or even if he has hurt his father deeply; the dad always has open arms.

Bel has a massive heart and is servant-hearted in her everyday life. She is loyal. I will always be grateful to her for simply inviting me, a stranger, into her home for dinner one evening.

The pink house was a place for broken people to come as they were, rest, and mend. The women who lived there were a part of a ministry called the "move-in" team. They also partnered with other ministry partners in the community to care for the people of East Vancouver and show them the love of Jesus.

One day Arely said to me, "healing happens in community." That is precisely what I came to know and experience there, more profoundly than I ever had before. It was in the daily interactions of grace and love in that home where my heart found healing.

The pink house ladies were the kind of people who give you the freedom to simply *be*. They opened their eyes, hands, and hearts to give the love they received from God. When I think back on my time in Vancouver, that is what I will never forget: those five women, God's provision over me, the fellowship, and the love that I was shown in that home.

The women who lived in the pink house had opportunities just like all of us to chase after worldly desires or things that would've made them look more "successful" to the world, but they chose to move into the pink house to serve Jesus in it and outside of it. I'm thankful to Christie and Arely, who said yes to the lovely pink house on Craigslist even though they had no idea how they were going to pay rent or how mightily God would use that one "yes." *"But God chose the foolish things of the world to shame the wise; God chose the weak things of the world to shame the strong"*

– 1st Corinthians 1:27 (NIV)

My naturopaths did proper testing, which showed that lyme had affected all systems of my body. They revealed to me through different tests how mold exposure had brutally affected my health. After doing different blood and urine tests, they told me that I had black mold inside my body.

Eric and Julie took action in treating the lyme right away through multiple treatment regimens paired with supportive therapies. They began the process of helping my body get rid of toxins through simple tools such as activated charcoal, which I surprisingly hadn't even heard of by any doctor before.

After all the testing, supplements, and treatments, my first week of treatment alone was over $2,000. This isn't uncommon for lyme patients. The initial appointments with lyme specialists and treatment protocol costs are typically out the window and not covered at all by insurance. This was obviously something I couldn't keep up with financially nor can anyone, even those with a regular 9-5 job and a good income.

Despite the obstacles to stay financially afloat and keep up with treatments, God's provision over me was undeniable every single day that I lived in Vancouver. From my naturopaths telling me not to worry about paying for various appointments, to my pretty friend with blonde dreads who didn't have much money yet was paying for my groceries, to the ticket machines on the bus being out of service when I didn't have enough money to ride, to someone I didn't know anonymously contributing $2,000 to my support site. The currency of Canada was also in my favor at the time, making about 75 cents in US currency become a dollar in Canadian money. God always met me wherever I was, and I never once ran out of money. Any time I even began to worry about not being able to pay for an IV or another form of treatment, God would provide.

After spending five unexpected months in Vancouver and experiencing physical healing like I never had before, I decided to buy a flight back to Tennessee. I was low in funds and thought that my health was in a stable enough place to get back to living a more "normal life." I thought the adventure was over.

I eventually met that pastor and his wife, who I was originally going to stay with in Vancouver. Oddly enough, I ate my first Canadian thanksgiving in their home. I had no idea that my friend who had invited me over was their son. It wasn't until someone said their names around the dinner table that it all clicked for me.

They were lovely. As I sat there at their table with a hilarious retired woman by the name of Margo to my left and the pastor's beautiful wife to my right, I was reminded of just how much had changed in my little world over the course of a couple of months. I had less pain in my body than I had in years, I realized that much of my mourning had turned to joy, and I was thankful.

I was thankful for the hard lessons, and I was struck with the reality that God truly did have something better in store for me back in August. The pink house was more fitting to my situation than anywhere else could be at the time.

One dreary afternoon a couple of days before leaving the pink house, I peeked out the window of my bedroom, silently reminiscing and reflecting on what that place meant to me. That room had been a place of restoration, hope, and refuge. At the same time, it had been a place of despair, defeat, and pain. It was filled with tears of confusion when symptoms got worse and tears of joy when another victory took place. Although a disease still lurked in my body, I had gained so much. I had the privilege of getting help from two brilliant and gifted specialists. I gained the strength to keep up the good fight. Most of all, though, I had gained much love. That right there, my friend, is priceless.

CHAPTER FOUR

Refined

"At least there is hope for a tree:
If it is cut down, it will sprout again,
and its new shoots will not fail.
Its roots may grow old in the ground
and its stump die in the soil,
yet at the scent of water it will bud
and put forth shoots like a plant."
Job 14 : 7-9 (NIV)

Have you ever lamented before the Lord? Have you ever wondered why He led you to something that caused you more pain? Have you ever cried out to Him and heard nothing but silence? I have.

Last night I lamented before the Lord. Then I felt guilty for lamenting because the night prior I had seen and felt Jesus and a very tall angel come to the foot of my bed and minister to me, and it felt disrespectful of me to say, "hey Jesus, I know that you came to me and sat on my bed last night, but it's not sufficient for me."

As I wept and got angry and laid it all out before Him, I thought to myself, "why are you here feeling sorry for yourself?" Then I felt God say, "that's what you needed yesterday. This is what you need today. You have to feel this now and get it out."

It would be quite whimsical if I reached the end of my lyme journey in Canada, and the rest was history. That I came back to Tennessee healed. That I got my life back. That there weren't any more health obstacles for me at such a young age. But what I didn't know was that there were years ahead of me that I'd barely be holding on. Yet God met me in profound ways during those years. He grew me into the woman I am today, and He healed some of my deepest wounds.

It wasn't long until after I moved back to Tennessee that my health rapidly declined again. A series of "randomness" occurred that eventually seemed way too coincidental and weird. For instance, the clinic in Nashville where I started receiving IVs had black mold all over the ceilings of the building (which was the last thing I wanted to be around after learning how much it had affected my health). Mind you, the mold was on the main floor, and the clinic was on an entirely different floor, but to me, mold was the scariest thing I could ever encounter at the time.

I reluctantly persisted because I knew those specific IVs had been vital in my healing for the last five months. After receiving a couple of IVs there, the receptionist told me that there was a shortage of sterilized water and that I temporarily couldn't get IVs. Soon after that, it was relayed to me that the owner of the clinic said that they were no longer permitted to treat me with no rhyme or reason as to why.

God's hand was on me then, even though it didn't feel like it. He was closing doors in Tennessee and opening doors back in Canada. So, I flew back to Vancouver, moved back into the pink house, and started treatment again. Unfortunately, I wasn't getting the results from treatment like I had the first time I lived there. Things weren't as fun and adventurous as before, either. And despite my efforts to pay for the treatments from working and fundraising, I couldn't keep up. So, I tried something new and cost-effective: bee venom therapy.

Bee venom is a form of treatment that has been successful for many lyme patients because venom from bees is proven to kill borrelia (yes, I got bee venom injected all over my back). Each session, we would up the injections of bee venom by two. It was somewhere between 12-16 injections along my spine all at once where my body began going into shock. I was herxing, and the adrenaline caused by the bee venom was too much on my system.

I'd never had a panic attack before then, but that is precisely what I began to experience after my last few sessions. Then came blood in my stools, no desire to eat, a gallbladder attack, and then my body feeling like it was shutting down. Dr. Moore insisted we stop treatment altogether. Déjà vu of other moments in other doctor's offices occurred as I sat in Dr. Moore's office and heard her say with tears in her eyes that she had no answers to why things had gotten so bad and had no idea what to do anymore.

It's mysterious how difficult circumstances can change us, for better or for worse. For better, they can allow us to become more resilient, refine our desires, and make us more grateful for what we have. Many other positive changes can take place. For worse, we can crumble under the weight of our challenging circumstances because we don't know how to give our burdens to God, and we don't know how to trust Him in our tragedies. Many other negative changes can take place, too.

Maybe there was purpose even in those moments that I didn't understand. God had placed me there in Canada again. He had given me those doctors. Maybe God wanted to reveal a little of His heart to those doctors through my life and maybe even more through my suffering. Maybe God was working on my own heart in the moments I didn't understand, the moments that forced me to rely on Him more.

As gratitude has been one of my greatest weapons throughout my healing journey, grieving has also been crucial to moving forward in a healthy way. Some things that seemed beyond obscure to grieve, I began to grieve after the whole bee venom fiasco. I realized that I hadn't allowed myself to do it as a child, so it was in my best interest to finally let myself go *there.*

Grief is a process. Though this tedious process of allowing ourselves to become detangled and completely undone to reveal the things we have been clenching for God knows how long is not easy by any means - it is crucial. Grieving can help your health and relationships tremendously. We may feel like we're not getting anywhere, but that's okay.

This is the process of healing, and it's good.

Depression's Strange Blessings

After stopping bee venom therapy and having no clear direction of what to do next, my body and brain weren't functioning the way they used to. I ached for any relief. I was weaker than usual, losing the few pounds I had left on my body and losing more mobility.

That Spring, I grew less desire to eat as most foods had lost their taste. I grew to hate the sun. All the things that were meant to bring healing and restoration felt like they were doing the opposite to my body, and I felt like I was going crazy. My body would randomly turn bright red all over, and my insides felt like they were on fire. I was going through the fire, quite literally.

I felt rigged and chilled to the bone. The walls around me that said security were crashing down, and my life felt sifted down into what felt like nothing. I had such faith that the bee venom protocol and the new antibiotics I was on would kill all the lyme spirochetes and help me get my life back as it had for so many others, but the opposite outcome had happened, and there were no answers.

Fear had sunken into my eyes. Although the people around me may not have seen it, I could feel it. Faith was one of those words I honestly got tired of hearing. I smiled less. When I did, I thought that the smile eased the vulnerable state of un-levelness where I was standing. I felt that the smile told people that I was okay - that I had my stuff together. That superficial smile was merely a facade and only kept me from allowing people in.

Many of the truths I'd been taught over the years were thrown out the window, and I was laid bare before God, just needing Him. I didn't want another scripture or a saying that would help me get through another day; I wanted God to tell me what was going on. I wondered why He wasn't comforting me and was confused as to why He was allowing me to suffer more.

As I cried out to God from under a white duvet cover and orange sheets that had been given to me, on a bed that had been given to me, I'd often catch myself staring at the wall next to my bed that had a window. I can still remember the details of that window and that wall. My greatest challenge was to keep having faith that wouldn't grow jaded or bitter. Every day was a fight for my life just as much as it was a fight against bitterness in my own heart and a fight against a downcast spirit.

I used to judge Christians with depression, especially those who had suicidal thoughts. I would think to myself, "they have Jesus, so why are they still depressed?" or "how could you ever be so selfish to think about committing suicide?" I don't think that way anymore. My eyes have been opened to how spiritual it is.

It all begins with the mind. That's how the enemy works. If he can get you to think a certain way, then he's got you where he wants you. "For as he thinks within himself, so he is." (from Proverbs 23:7 NAS).

The depression that I faced felt like a mixed outcome of my present life spilling out like fresh tar over former things that I had never grieved as a kid. My brain was struggling to compute how to cope anymore. Like most kids, I couldn't process the difficult things that happened during my childhood, and that weight carried on into adulthood.

There were angels in the form of people who walked into my life during those five desolating months. One day, I met a woman named Holly. Holly lived in a bold, yellow-colored house. Her home was conveniently located a block away from the pink house, on the corner across from a cozy cafe and coffee shop called the Wilder Snail.

Holly has elegant eyes and a soft, giggly face. Holly is one of those moms that gets in the dirt with her kiddos and allows them to roll in the mud butt naked and let the mud dry into dirt. She allows her kids to run, jump, laugh, and make forts with their friends in the living room. Holly is content spending the whole day in a community garden down the street with her two blonde mop-headed angels. Holly is one of my favorite moms because of the way I see her love her kids.

Lauren lived in a blue house with a red door. She and her husband Chris are filmmakers and producers in Vancouver. Lauren is one of the most rad moms I know - full of bravery, creativity, and humility. She is sheerly real and authentic. Lauren found me on a website where I was listed as a caregiver, invited me into her home, and the next day, she hired me to take care of her sweet baby girl who was six months old at the time – Georgia (AKA baby G) for a couple hours in the afternoon while she was working.

I watched Lauren allow her baby girl to fall, get back up again, and grow. Lauren lovingly held her precious Georgia loosely, entrusting her into my arms every day at noon. Baby G had eyes that you'd get lost in every time you get a glimpse of them. I loved those eyes. Baby G helped me see the beauty and frailty of life; Baby G brought me tremendous joy.

Grace is another magnificent human being. Grace once shared some of her testimony at Adria's church after Adria had preached about the prostitute at Jesus' feet. As Grace stood on that stage, she explained how she had been raped as a child and a young woman and then went on to explain how her wounds don't define her. Grace is incredible.

I'm thankful for all the angels that walked into my life during that season, even when I kept shutting my door and shutting my heart. I am thankful to the pink house ladies who continued to pray for me and be there for me through it all. I won't forget what Holly, Lauren, and other women taught me then about motherhood as they faced each day with creativity and love. They taught me that it isn't about being perfect or having it all together. It's about being present.

Necessary Growth

It's a painful process when all the layers around your heart that have been built on lies become exposed. It's painful being refined. As the Refiner chisels away at you in the fire, you change. You become stronger and more beautiful inside.

I reached the point where getting up the stairs became too difficult, so the couch in the living room became my bed. The couch was right next to the front door of the pink house. So, every time someone would walk through that door, I felt like I was on display. I didn't want to be seen in my suffering.

Feeling like a burden had become so familiar to me, making it very difficult to receive another ounce of help from people. My friend, Christie, looked past all my broken filters and loved me like a sister. She cared for me when I was too weak to take care of myself.

All I honestly thought I wanted in life was to be healthy again. Part of that was true - I *was* disappointed that treatment made me feel worse. I *was* disappointed that there was still no cure or that even with all the knowledge I had gained, even with the strict diet that I was on, even with the care of great doctors - I still wasn't well.

What I didn't realize then was that the desires of my heart were still in need of refining. I don't say that to say that God refrained from healing me in order that my heart be more refined; I say it simply as a fact. I had this idea of working at a coffee shop, finally having the freedom to buy a little bit edgier clothes than I had like those holey jeans that were really "in" and posting cool pictures on my instagram that all my friends back home would tap to like. Then I would, in turn, feel more validated about where I was at in life. I imagined being some girl from Tennessee who lives in a pink house and goes to a "cool church."

It feels so shallow saying it now, but it was true. At 22 years old, I wanted the instant gratification that this world is quick to hand over to me if I asked it to. I looked on social media, all the manipulation, flaunting, replicating – and I was intrigued. I wanted to be liked by people, and I struggled against the shallowness that I saw myself and some of my friends falling into. This isn't to say that social media is bad or evil - I see many people using it for good. But whenever I find myself aimlessly scrolling through social media, it's typically because I'm subconsciously trying to avoid something hard in my own life.

I forgot about my identity in Christ and all the delightful things He says about me. I forgot that my life could never be defined by little squares on a screen, what kind of job I had, or whether I had a disease or not. I forgot about God's vision for my life and that being dependent on Him is the best place to be.

Refinement is the process of removing impurities or unwanted elements from a substance. Other words used for refinement are cleansing, clarification, filtering, and treatment. I find it ironic that treatment is a synonym of refinement, because all my lyme disease treatments have felt like physical representations of what's been taking place inside me all these years: refinement.

Refinement takes place in some of the most majestic and expensive items in the world - gold, diamonds, and pearls, to name a few. All must undergo refinement to become the final product. If they don't go through the fire, they don't turn out right. And ironically, the refinement makes them more beautiful.

The refiner's fire is necessary. Being refined like fire and tested like gold makes us more pliable. But more than anything, the refiner's fire is a chance for us to grow in the character of Christ.

Most of those days seemed to serve no purpose, but deep down, I know that they needed to happen. I had to stop being identified with a disease. Yes, I had it still, but I had to learn that it wasn't a part of my identity. Lyme had taken the front seat of my life over the past year, and I needed to be reminded that it wasn't who I was.

Some seasons are meant to be seasons of lament. Sometimes you must give your heart the permission to be saturated in sadness. Let the flood of grief in your heart rise and show itself. Let the sadness you've been pushing away say what it needs to say.

My heart started to say what it needed to say during those rainy days. I never understood depression or anxiety growing up, but now I did. And because I understood it more, there was no longer internal judgment every time I heard a friend say they were struggling with depression, but instead an open conversation and a chance to pray for them.

Looking back, I'm so thankful for that season. I'm so grateful that God saved me from superficiality and made me a healthier person emotionally and mentally. I'm so grateful that my hardships allowed my roots to go deeper.

One morning after experiencing piercing pain in my abdomen for days on end, I woke up with less pain than I had all week. I felt the mercy of God pouring out on me in that same bed with those orange sheets and that white duvet that had been given to me. The words that bled into my heart upon waking were, *"I am with you to the very end, Lo."*

I wish that I could say that I quickly turned to God in all those moments where He was so gracious with me, but if

I'm honest with myself, I didn't always do that. I was often wallowing in doubt that anything would ever change. Yet Jesus was present in that room, in that bed, on those old, intricate wooden floors of the pink house; even when I wasn't inviting Him in, and I saw new depths of His compassion and grace amid my shallowness. I'm so thankful that God invited me to live a life beyond mediocre, a life beyond myself. I'm so thankful that He invited me to a life of refinement.

Before moving back to Canada, I thought the part of my journey where "I have lyme disease" was nearly over. I felt so ready to be independent. I didn't want to be the girl at another gathering who had to lie down the whole time because of the pain I was in. I was tired of being weak and asking people and even Jesus for help most days.

As much as I wanted lyme to be over, that part of my journey was the part that made me more of who I think I was always meant to become. There was so much more depth to my life than before all the suffering. I may have been sicker in my body, but I had grown. I had new faces that God led me to who became like family to me, and, through all the messiness: my heart had been continuing to heal - which I think is a greater healing than a physical healing would've been.

Cracks and Waves

After a storm one day, the wall next to my bed in my room at the pink house that I often stared at had developed bigger cracks than before. The wall was primitive, the kind you see in an old home full of elaborate crown molding, massive windows with their original glass, and with hallways full of glazy wooden floors that you slid down in your fuzzy socks as a kid. The wall in my room may have looked damaged and some may have said that it was in need of repair, but it was less ordinary than before. It had more character.

The cracks on that wall reminded me of the cracks in my

own life that had created more character in me. A crack can cause immense pain to the whole wall in the moment, and yet that crack is what I run my fingers over today as I feel those odd imperfections that I've grown to appreciate on that wall. The cracks may look messy, but I praise God for them. He has filled the cracks with abundantly more meaning and worth than if the crack had never formed. The cracks are the good stuff.

Someone I met in Trinidad and Tobago while on my DTS outreach once told me that she pictured me in an ocean while praying for me. She said that the waves would not stop taking me underwater. That's how my life has felt ever since.

Illness that goes on for years feels like you're being taken under waves every day without your consent or will. As I'm underwater, bearing the weight of another wave that's pulling my limbs in all directions, I solemnly say to God, "I need air. Will you finally give me some air?" Sometimes He gives me air, and sometimes He allows another wave. My friend Sam who also got diagnosed with lyme, recently said this at a bible study: "the wave that the enemy meant to drown you with, God is using to baptize you in His love."

Maybe you, too, feel as if the waves will never stop. When those waves come rushing in over us, we search for anything that looks safe. We want to be comforted under the waves. We want stability. We may even dig our toes in the sand to gain some sense of control, but we're frankly trapped and trying not to become frantic over how out of control we are.

There is something else I see unveiling in those moments, though. God's allowing us to know Him more. Under those waves, you and I have an opportunity to gain a little more trust in Jesus. Jesus, the author and finisher of our faith. Jesus, our most sincere friend.

We can't let the waves toss and turn us wherever they please. We must hold onto our anchor, Jesus. No matter how crazy those waves get, our anchor isn't going anywhere.

We stay grounded in Him as we keep holding onto Him.

I know when I spend a whole day out in the ocean, my sandy body is utterly exhausted whenever it makes its way back to the hotel room. It's a good kind of exhaustion, though. I'm exhausted and exhilarated at the same time. I'm thinking more clearly, and I'm feeling more confident about the future.

Now, if I were to keep going out into the ocean and getting hit by the waves every day for the next decade, that exhaustion would seem overpowering, and that exhilaration would no longer feel existent. That's how lyme disease that doesn't go away feels. But somewhere, underneath all that exhaustion and whiplash, after all those waves, as Jesus leads me back to stable ground, I'm more alive in a soberly kind of way. I'm also more grounded in who I'm called to be, because Jesus was there with me in all those waves - even if I didn't see Him.

"The LORD is close to the brokenhearted and saves those who are crushed in spirit" - Psalm 34:18 (NIV)

CHAPTER FIVE
Unbeaten Paths

"Not only so, but we also glory in our sufferings, because
we know that suffering produces perseverance;
perseverance, character; and character, hope. And hope
does not put us to shame, because God's love has been
poured out into our hearts through the Holy Spirit, who
has been given to us." Romans 5:3-5 (NIV)

Ever since I can remember, I've enjoyed stepping onto
unbeaten paths. Off the sidewalks, off the grid, into the
woods, underneath the pine trees that oozed out their
sugary sap onto my hands. Places where I can breathe a little
deeper and worry a little less. I can recall countless moments
as a kid getting wrapped up in nature so deeply that I'd climb
up trees too high to get down from, accidentally run into
skunks, with bats grazing over my head, or a chipmunk
climbing up my leg - all the while, I just kept trekking along
the woods of Michigan, oblivious to what was going on or
what could lie ahead.

I'm still a bit like that kid. I still step on unfamiliar and
unmarked paths that aren't typically where my friends are
going. Maybe you've also walked some unbeaten paths that

not many people you know have walked, or you've encountered experiences that not many people you know have encountered. Though these paths can be lonely and painful, they can be unbelievably rewarding. I see my unbeaten paths as anthems that shout God's faithfulness from the rooftops of my heart and shoot the enemy right back down to his place.

If there's one thing that I want to testify about every day for the rest of my life, I think it'd be about the faithfulness of God. He's been faithful in every season. His continual provision has been indisputable. He's also added some humor, adventures, and traveling along the way because He knows that I enjoy all those things.

That Spring, months after stopping bee venom therapy and still not recovering, I met a funny Canadian lady named Dawn. Holly, my friend that lived in the yellow house, mentioned that she had a friend with lyme whose whole family had been horrifically affected by it. Holly suggested that the three of us have breakfast together at her place.

The day I met Dawn was a good day. I was at a loss of what to do for treatment, but like He always does, God sent someone else to help me. I felt the presence of God as I sat there at Holly's table surrounded by two non-Christians who were showing me God's love without even knowing it.

Dawn proceeded to share chunks of information on lyme that I was unaware of. She also invited me to come with her to Seattle to sit in on her consultation with a highly recommended lyme specialist who charged over $800 to see for a consultation alone. Before I knew it, I found myself in a car with someone whom I'd just met crossing the border back to America – to meet another lyme specialist.

After he consulted Dawn, this specialist walked up to me and kindly said in his cute European accent, "you are going to get well." He encouraged me to get my tonsils and teeth checked. He also advised me to get tested for parasites. I believe the Lord gave this man insight into my situation. On our car ride back up to Canada, Dawn and I laughed uncontrollably and talked about all that we faced in our battle with lyme disease (how refreshing it is to relate with others going through the same thing). That day was special, maybe even monumental, because I was experiencing something I hadn't felt in a long time: *hope*.

About a week later, I tagged along with Dawn across the border and into Seattle to meet another naturopath that had helped Dawn exponentially. That naturopath had worked vigorously to treat her own chronic health issues years ago and was now doing the same for many others through unique alternative forms of medicine.

During my appointment with Dawn's naturopath, she discovered something new that hadn't ever been addressed by medical professionals I had worked with before. Unbeknownst to me, my jaw had been chronically infected for years. She believed that having such a big infection in my body was deteriorating my health and making it impossible for my immune system to simultaneously fight off lyme successfully.

Finally, I had more answers to the root of the problem. I only had a couple of connections in Seattle, but I knew that it was my next step toward healing. It was time to get fresh eyes on my medical case, and I knew the only way to go forward was to keep trying new forms of treatment.

Upon arriving back in Canada, I decided to buy a bus ticket and make my way down to my next open door. The morning I left the pink house, I still can recall feeling defeat, shame, and thinking that I had somehow failed because I wasn't healed yet. Wondering, *"what was the point of all of this?"* God didn't blame me or shame me that day, nor does He ever. He sat with me.

A few hours later, I was in Seattle – the place I had no idea God would keep proving His kindness to me for the next seven months. As I stood there across the street from an unfamiliar train station, as the sun beamed on my face and my big red suitcase that was probably tired of traveling and being overstuffed, I began to ponder what in the world

I was doing or how I ended up in Seattle out of all places in the world. That was when a generous and courageous woman named Claire came rushing in.

Claire goes the extra mile for people she doesn't even know; take me for instance. She came and picked me up in her shiny white car on that warm day in May, having never met me and knowing very little information about me from Lauren, baby G's mom, who had previously reached out to Claire about my situation. Claire welcomed me into her gorgeous modern home on a hill in the suburbs of Seattle and told me that I was welcome to stay there with their adorable golden retriever for ten days while she was away with her husband and son.

When Claire and her family got back from their trip, she reassured me that I was free to stay in their home for a longer period of time. Claire and Jason weren't believers, but they showed me the love of God. As I continued treatment and God continued to open doors, I found myself now unexpectedly living in Seattle.

Germany Bound

Before moving to Seattle and working with a new naturopath, I thought nothing of all the multiple failed root canals I had as a teenager or how they would all somehow end up infected only for dentists to redo and use more toxic materials in the process. Those materials shouldn't be used on someone who is immune-compromised and has had all the dental issues I've had. Sadly, by the time I became educated on the potential side effects of poor dental work, the damage had already been done.

My naturopath in Seattle said that the only person who she believed would remove the infection and heavy metals from my mouth correctly and successfully was Dominick Nischwitz, who happened to be conveniently located in Germany out of all places. He had an outstanding reputation and used non-toxic materials that no dentists in the states used.

The specific procedure I needed to fix the catastrophes on both sides of my mouth without exposing myself to more toxicity would cost between €8,000-10,000 (euros). It was pricey, but still plenty cheaper than what other holistic dentists in America were telling me their rates were for the same surgery and who weren't as advanced as Dominick. As difficult as it was to wrap my mind around flying across the globe for a dental procedure, it seemed to be the next logical step to take. Contrarily, flying across the world in the shape I was in did not seem logical at all.

I called one of my closest pals at the time, Bex, who lived in England. She was like, "wait, so you're going to Germany to get a surgery, and you don't even know their language? How are you going to get around or get food?" I guess I hadn't thought it through that far.

For nearly three years, Bex and I had planned to spend a summer together in Africa. I had to eventually pull out of the plan because I wasn't better like I had hoped and expected to be by then. Instead of being upset that I couldn't follow through on our dream to spend a summer in Africa, she decided that she wanted to spend the little money she had to fly from her home in England to come to Germany and take care of me the week of my surgery. Bex had very little, yet she chose to selflessly use that little to help me.

So, I had a friend willing to come take care of me, and I found another insanely cheaply priced flight this time across the globe, but I still had no funds for the actual surgery. I was willing to go into debt for it, but there was still an upfront payment of over $6,000 that the dentist's office in Germany was asking for that I didn't have. As I prepared for my trip and continued to fundraise on my support site, I still wasn't sure if flying to Germany for a procedure for which I currently had none of the money for was an act of stupidity or faith.

As always, God provided for every need. When Bex and I met up in Germany, our friend Chrissy picked us up from the airport. We had all become friends years prior when we lived in Mexico together. Chrissy drove us to our Airbnb hours away and helped us out tremendously during the duration of the trip.

The day before the surgery, Dr. Dominik asked me how I was going to pay. I can't remember exactly what came out of my mouth, but I do remember that by God's grace, I was filled with faith and belief that the money was going to flood in somehow. That evening, one of my friends got on my support site and told me that he had a "chunk of change" that he had saved during college, which was much more than just a chunk of change. He had anonymously contributed over $6,000. Then another friend donated online that same night. Both friends told me that they felt God leading them to give the rest of what I needed, and I mean the exact amount.

Unexpected Healing from My Father

I was not aware that, in Europe, it's not common to go under for an eight-hour procedure. So even though I begged for it, I didn't get the laughing gas. Then the anesthesia didn't work. No matter how much Dominick numbed my mouth during the surgery, I had continuous spouts of shooting pains down the left side of my jaw and entire body.

At one point during the procedure, I suddenly became emotional, and I didn't understand why. Dominick asked if I wanted a brief break which I quickly accepted. Just a few moments later, he peeked his head in the door and reminded me to think positively. I knew at that moment that simply thinking positively was not what I was supposed to do. I knew God was telling me at that moment that we were going to the very root - the deepest roots of my pain - and to allow Him to heal it.

There in that room, all alone, I wept. I grieved what I never allowed myself to grieve - yes, oddly enough during a dental surgery on the other side of the world. I felt the Lord say to me that my earthly father did not know how to love his daughters the way God intended him to, and I grieved that. I grieved the trauma from a man I was meant to trust abusing me instead.

That day, my true Dad came through for me in ways I won't ever forget. I was reminded that the brokenness in my father and I's relationship had been a catalyst to running to my ultimate Father more and experiencing a deeper relationship with Him in ways I don't think would've been possible without the wounds from my earthly dad. I wouldn't have known the depths of my true Father's love because I wouldn't have sought it out as desperately. My identity as a true daughter of God had to be ingrained into the depths of me because I had no other option if I was going to keep believing in God.

I was reminded that my earthly father has brokenness, as we all do. He never got to heal, and I had to keep extending forgiveness and grace to him. That forgiveness and grace is the same forgiveness and grace that has allowed my true Father to heal me as I've laid on His chest and have been held by Him.

When Dominick came back to continue the procedure, another out-of-the-ordinary occurrence took place. As I continued to experience relentless pain in my jaw, he began to pull a giant cyst out of my left jaw. He said that the cyst, which I had no idea was there, had a nervous system of its own and was the reason why I was experiencing so much pain. As soon as he removed the cyst, the rest of the procedure went smoothly.

The cyst felt like a representation of all the pain my father had caused me. It was invisible, and yet it had its own nervous system. It was controlling how my entire body was responding. That's how trauma works. You can be completely removed from a situation, and yet you can still act as if you're in that situation without even realizing it. Your body still remembers how traumatic it was, and your nervous system still responds the same way it did while you were in trauma. Yet that cyst, that host of unwanted trauma, is wreaking havoc on me. It must be recognized for what it is and brought into the light. It needs the hands of the only one who can do the job right - the Surgeon - to come in and pluck it out.

My trip to Germany was a peculiar experience that I still can't quite put into words, but what matters is that God showed Himself faithful in miraculous ways. Being awake during that eight-hour procedure was a bit of an analogy of what true healing in our lives legitimately looks like. It's painful, uncomfortable, long, and even dreadful at times. It's a place you're scared of going. Yet as you are forced to stay present and alert through the entire process, God reveals Himself to you and heals you in the places you need it most - whether you're aware you need healing in those places or not.

Dr. Dominick was exceptional that week, driving me to and from my Airbnb to his office and checking in with me every step of the way. At the end of the surgery, Dominick told me that he wanted to take thousands of euros off the initial price for me, saying that it was his own "fundraiser" for me. As if that wasn't enough, my Canadian friend Dawn who originally connected me with the doctor who connected me to this dentist, asked me one day over the phone where I would most want to go after Germany. I said Tennessee.

Dawn hung up and called her brother, who I've never met, and asked if he could buy me a flight to Tennessee with his mileage points. The next day a guy I'd never talked to before gave me a flight across the globe for free.

Within a span of less than three weeks, I stayed in three different countries, eight different homes, and I had little to no sleep for many days. With not much energy to do much of anything, God placed people right in front of me who were in need of something (or Someone to be more accurate) so much more valuable than my physical healing ever would be. I needed money and medical care, but these people were in need of Jesus. I was reminded that all I could offer was love, and I witnessed the power of God invade my new friends and me in some of our weakest moments.

At The Feet of Jesus

The day after my dental surgery, I felt scared, oppressed, and angry. Everything felt dark. I had never experienced anything quite like it. According to Dominick, I was dumping loads of heavy metals and toxins out of my body after the surgery, and the antibiotic that he had injected into my jaw was making me feel even more awful - if that was possible.

I try to look back on that time with lightness and comedy, but it was not any of that at the moment. I was not myself. That's when I discovered the remarkable benefits of chlorella for the first time. Chlorella is an algae binder that proved effective and was a game-changer for me when detoxing heavy metals. It has been one of the most helpful supplements I've regularly taken ever since.

The surgery seemed to only open the door to more pain, and I didn't know how to endure it anymore. I remembered the words of people I looked up to and how they learned how to heal themselves. I admired many of these people, but I knew that even if I gained all the knowledge that the world had to offer about my condition, some things were simply too grand for me to comprehend. My healing was in God's hands.

But I was tired of waiting on Him, tired of getting my hopes up, tired of taking steps of faith for things that didn't make any sense or have the outcome that I was hoping for. But God met me again. Alone in a room of an empty house in Tübingen, Germany that my friend and I had been given to stay by people we'd never met, I sensed the Father saying, "It's not about how you handle this, but about me, your Provider, meeting you in all of it."

Isn't that the truth? Jesus is the one who shines His light and glory over all our messiness. It isn't about getting up off the floor and picking up all the pieces. Instead, it's about taking the focus and the pressure off ourselves and throwing everything we feel at the feet of Jesus, where He then creates a stupendous masterpiece out of our broken pieces - in due time.

Gudrun

When I returned to Seattle, I was not recovering from surgery like we had hoped or feeling any better for that matter. On the contrary, I was feeling much worse.

I didn't have a place to stay, but I knew that I had to continue treatment if I ever wanted my life back. I took a ferry out to a stunning place called Bainbridge Island, where my friend Lauren - another one of the girls I lived with in Panama - had kindly offered me to come stay in her lofty home with her.

I was continually blown away by people's generosity to me in Seattle. After staying with Lauren, my naturopath offered me to stay in her old apartment that she no longer lived in but was still paying rent on until the end of the month. I don't know many people who would do that. My naturopath was also kind enough to call one of her other patients, Gudrun, and ask if I could stay with her when I needed a place to stay. A few days later, I called Gudrun. In her endearing German-drawn voice, she told me to come and stay at her house on Mercer Island whenever I wanted to.

The moment that my friend Lulu and I opened the wooden gate and approached her home, there we saw the elegant beaming face of little Gudrun standing in the doorway with her bright blue wooden front door open. Gudrun was a splendid 84-year-old lady full of passion, love, sass, and stories. Lots of stories. Gudrun's husband, Jack, had passed away a few years back after a long battle with lyme. Gudrun spoke with such tenderness and admiration of her husband, who she had taken care of for over ten years while his health progressively declined.

Gudrun allowed me to stay in her sophisticated home

with her too many nights to count. She offered me food when she herself was struggling in her speech, along with a plethora of other debilitating symptoms from lyme. I saw a woman who had been through horrific things, yet so much about her demeanor was still soft and lovely. She had some grit and feistiness in her, too.

Gudrun became my closest friend in Seattle. I began to cherish all the mundane moments with that cute, short, comical woman. I'll never forget laughing with my old lady friend over the weird things that lyme disease did to our bodies. Even if the laughing masked the pain, God was giving me life, and I was thankful to still be able to laugh.

I remember one week where I spent many hours in a bed in Gudrun's guest room, many moments of agony, discouragement, barely speaking a word all day because I was at a loss for words. I was broken before the Lord. Yet, he had given me friends. I had Gudrun by my side as we shared stories with one another and shared in one another's suffering.

Sitting with Gudrun was something in and of itself that taught me more than almost anything else in life at 23 years old. I guess it was the way of life she exuded that I wanted. She was suffering so deeply yet had the most adorable little walk and talk and style of an 84-year-old woman.

You live at a different pace of life when you are in the presence of Gudrun. She stoops down to pick up another plum that fell from her plum tree, then we sit on her porch, with no agenda for the day. The sun beams on her face, and she begins to tell me all about her tomato plant in front of us. The seeds of this plant were the last thing she can remember from her brother in Germany before he passed away.

She holds my hand while we walk, and she tells me a little more about Jack, the man who she had loved for so many years. She isn't broken, she's still kickin'. She knows that her time on earth isn't up yet. And I realized that for the rest of my life, I want to surround myself with the rare amount of people in the world like Gudrun.

I hope to be like the stoic angel by the name of Gudrun one day. I hope to be like Jell-O when I'm old: soft, goofy, and transparent. I want to be someone that kids look forward to being around. One who has let go of what people think about her; who hasn't allowed bitterness into her heart no matter how much it could be justified. The kind of lady who takes an 11-hour plane ride across the world at 84 years old - *yes, Gudrun did that.*

Gudrun was one of the bravest women I've ever known. Her arm was broken, her speech and sight failed at times, yet she remained hopeful. Gudrun and I walked around her garden full of vibrantly colored tomatoes, pears, and raspberries. She held my hand tightly. With tears in her eyes of tenderness, she said, "we will get through this."

She was right. You and I will get through whatever we face because God has us. For my friends who are beyond weary in your trials, beyond weary in asking your community for help, He has not forgotten us. He is with us, and no matter how hardened our hearts feel at this moment, what I say is true. What matters at the end of the day is that our hearts are soft before our Savior.

Continuous Provision

It's mind-blowing to me how God's family is everywhere. My friend Bri from Tennessee has a friend named Rachel who lived a ferry ride away from Seattle in Silverdale, Washington. Soon after moving to Seattle, I became pals with Rachel and her husband, Jeff. They connected me with their church, where Rachel shared my story and told them that I was looking for housing. As soon as they heard my story, a cute Korean couple named Ivy and Sung offered me to stay with them in their clean mold-free home. After staying with Ivy and Sung for a month, God's provision over me still abounded to my surprise.

Rachel and Jeff's church slowly became my community. Mosaic church embraced me, and I was never without. I stayed in other people's homes besides Ivy and Sung's while I lived in Seattle, including Rachel and Jeff, as well as my kind friends Audrey and Pete, who graciously let me stay in their cozy guest room.

On one sunny day at the end of August when I was so over asking for help, nearly at the point of packing my bag to fly back to Nashville and give up, out of nowhere, I got a call from a woman that I had met once briefly in passing named Dawn. Dawn was the mom of another friend of a friend whom I had just met named Kimberly. Kimberly and her husband had just had me over for lunch after my friend Bex had connected us.

Dawn told me on that phone call that her husband, herself, and a girl named Erin, who was living with them, wanted to extend the invitation to come live with them free of charge until I finished treatment. Wow. To say that God had his hand over me in Seattle is an understatement. Dawn and her husband lived in the same town as my naturopath did, so that meant no more hours of public transit. No more hopping around. No more wondering where I was going to live again in order to keep getting treatment. Dawn, Mark, and Erin were a grand answer to prayer. Tears fell down my face when we got off the phone, and as I sat there on that bed, I was astonished that after all of this time, still, God was taking care of me.

Physical Healing Wasn't the Point

"For this reason I kneel before the Father, from whom every family in heaven and on earth derives its name. I pray that out of his glorious riches he may strengthen you with power through his Spirit in your inner being, so that Christ may dwell in your hearts through faith. And I pray that you, being rooted and established in love, may have power, together with all the Lord's holy people, to grasp how wide and long and high and deep is the love of Christ, and to know this love that surpasses knowledge—that you may be filled to the measure of all the fullness of God.

74

Now to him who is able to do immeasurably more than all we ask or imagine, according to his power that is at work within us, to him be glory in the church and in Christ Jesus throughout all generations, for ever and ever! Amen." Ephesians 3:14-21 (NIV)

One warm day in September, a few months after my procedure in Germany and lyme still making every day a daunting challenge, God spoke to me. Nothing crazy, just a few simple words that I needed to hear in that season. As I was getting out of my uber for another appointment with my naturopath, I felt the Lord gently yet firmly rebuke me in my spirit with, "stop relying on her and start depending on Me." I abruptly and awkwardly walked back outside just before my appointment. I hadn't realized that I had slowly come to rely on the physician in front of me more for my physical healing than I was relying on my ultimate Physician for it.

I got out in nature and found a field to sit in surrounded by pretty views. This town, Woodinville, which had become my home, was full of breath-taking trails, wineries, open areas, and my favorite little lavender farm. As I sat there in my conviction, God was calling me to go deeper with Him in ways I had not gone before.

I called and confided in my friend Christie about what I felt the Lord was speaking. She then asked me if there was anyone in the world who I felt like I should get prayed over. At first, I thought, "hundreds of people have prayed for me; why would I go ask someone else to pray over me?" I guess after seeking out prayer from so many people for so many years and not getting better, I was probably jaded. But my friend knew that what I needed was a move of God in my life. Not more supplements or more forms of treatment, but healing that only God could perform. I then thought of a man named Todd White, a man who I have always looked up to. For years, I had randomly had dreams of him praying for me.

I found online that Todd was going to be teaching a class that he helped lead and teach, and the next one was going to be held in California in a couple weeks. Before I knew it, I found myself on a $177 round trip to California, where I attended a four-day class with my friend, who I had to thank for the whole idea. Christie ended up surprising me there in Bakersfield, California - which I hear has been nicknamed the armpit of America. So the trip was not glamorous by any stretch, but that didn't matter to my friend. She didn't want to miss seeing me get healed.

During those four days, many people prayed over me, including Todd. On the very last night of the event, right after Todd walked off the stage, I called out his name as I struggled to make my way to him. He asked me what I needed prayer for, and I answered with lyme disease.

He looked into my eyes with the love of God, said, "I love you," and then prayed for me. I don't remember anything he said when he was praying, only what was happening before my eyes. As he prayed, I noticed my friend beside me genuinely crying over my pain and over her desire for my healing.

I then heard the following words from a still small voice ring in my heart, words that turned my world upside down. I heard, "it's not about the healing, but about people knowing My love." Those words changed my life. I was reminded at that moment that the people God has placed in my life are way more precious than any physical healing ever could be, and I was reminded that I could still be a vessel of God's love even if I was still sick.

Hearing the gentle voice of my Savior changes me. His words shift my perspective. Hearing words straight from His heart gives me the ability to walk away from situations that could've been detrimental disappointments but instead, I have joy, peace, and more desire for Jesus. When I get a deeper revelation of the Lord's love over me, I am changed, and I have more love for the people around me. I can speak into the lives of others around me better because I've been touched by the King of Kings. Physical healing will be great when it happens, but I think a more remarkable thing can take place in the suffering: that we would grasp how wide and long and high and deep is the fiery love of God.

In hindsight, I think my favorite part of that trip was the moment I saw my friend in a window of a greyhound bus station in Bakersfield, CA, with a little backpack and a whole lot of love. Christie was ready to walk those four days out with me, regardless of whatever the outcome would be. She had decided to come all the way from Canada just to be there and support me. I was shocked by her investment of time and money and her desire to simply see me get healed.

I was reminded of how healing friendship can be and humbled by someone sewing so much of it into my life. I was inspired. My friend so willingly entered into my suffering over and over again ever since I had met her, and I remembered how important *that* is to Jesus. *Entering into people's suffering* is one of the most spectacular things we can do for one another.

CHAPTER SIX
Beneath The Surface

"As you do not know the path of the wind, or how the
body is formed in a mother's womb, so you cannot
understand the work of God, the Maker of all things"
Ecclesiastes 11:5 (NIV)

"You are healed!!!" I would hear another person say as I
prepared to walk back to my seat after walking forward at
church asking for prayer. Over the years, I've hundreds of
people put their hands on me and pray over me, some with
names that many in the Christian community know or at
least have heard of. Many of these prayers from people's
hearts have touched my own heart in massive ways. On the
contrary, some have felt more like a shame fest or blaming
me for why I hadn't been healed yet. I've had multiple
people say that one of my legs was growing out and
proclaim out to the entire church there on the stage that I
was healed. But again, my legs were not a different length to
begin with, and again, I felt more discouraged than anything
walking away from those prayers.

If I was feeling brave enough that day to be completely
honest with them, I would say something like, "I don't feel

better," or "the pain hasn't improved." They would reply with, "well, you are healed!!" Posting pictures of me on social media, telling everyone that I had been healed after they had prayed for me... God bless all of them. I must have grace on all of them. We are all growing in the Lord, and something that can be damaging to one person can be the exact words that someone else needs to hear, the exact prayer that sets someone free.

...It was damaging to my spirit at times, though. Many times, after leaving my church or another friend's church where there had been someone who wanted to pray for me, as I would declare and believe but not get better, I would be left alone with a silent aching that I concluded needed to be hidden between God and me. Those experiences left me confused and sometimes in even more denial about the condition I was still in.

I have many friends who have walked away from the church because the church did not know how to handle their suffering. One of my friends who has chronic illness was told that she "wasn't being a good role model for the teenagers" and was asked to step down from her role after she had to stay home sick from church and not volunteer at a youth group. People in her small group made jokes about her husband getting sick of dealing with her problems and insinuated that he should leave her. When she had to cancel plans with new friends from church due to an ER visit, they called her and her husband "flakey."

I have another friend who battled an eleven-year-long journey against chronic lyme that completely altered his life, his wife's life, and his three kids' lives. What he constantly went through had him not wanting to live anymore. He's just now starting to rebuild his life, but there are still many scars.

Once while visiting his mom, she insisted that he come along with her to church even though he was in debilitating pain and "wasn't feeling up to it" would be an understatement. He went to church, where his mom then asked him to lead the time of prayer. As you can imagine, naturally, the last thing he wanted to do was get up and lead a congregation in prayer. So, he got up there and faked the whole thing with a smile on his face.

Experience had taught my friend that it was easier to fake it in front of the church than be honest about what he was going through. He knew that if he got up there and shared what he was enduring and the serious needs that he had, there probably would've been crickets.

These stories are not constricted to people with chronic illness. I have a friend who struggled with infertility for years and some of the comments I heard some people in the church say to her were absurd. What is it about long-term suffering that makes us so uncomfortable? Why do we feel the need to have all the answers instead of just listening to people and meeting them where they're at? Maybe sometimes certain forms of suffering are a sober reminder that we are all one diagnosis, one car crash, one phone call away from complete tragedy. We don't want to be reminded of this reality.

Many people in the church have said words that have made me feel agonizing shame for still being sick. They believed that if we just pray the stripes of Jesus over ourselves until we are blue in the face that we will always be healed. That the healing solely depends on our faith. And if we aren't healed, it's only because of a lack in our own faith.

The stripes of Jesus are my healing. I still believe that. I still proclaim that. Darkness cannot stand against the blood of Jesus. But I do not condemn people for their sicknesses or tell them that if they just try harder or proclaim something more that they will be healed. Maybe God is withholding or delaying for a reason. Maybe He's writing a unique story in someone's life that permits suffering in order to fulfill His purposes.

Our intentions may be so pure and good, but a physical healing is not for us to ultimately determine or to hand out reasons as to why it has or hasn't happened. This isn't to say that there aren't things we can't control like our prayer life, our attitude, our mindset, our diet, among many other things that help our health exponentially. This is also not to say that our prayers don't make a difference or that God doesn't bring people miraculous healings through our hands, which can happen at any moment! But, if someone is still hurting after I've prayed for them, I don't tell them that they are healed. I see the best things happen when I simply sit with them and allow the Lord to lead me.

The reality is that we all will fail one another to a degree. Without Jesus, I have nothing substantial or dense to offer people. God is the only one who can do for them exactly what they need and to the degree that they need. If He wants to use me in the process, hallelujah.

The Trailblazer
"Consider Him, who endured such opposition from sinners, so that you will not grow weary and lose heart" Hebrews 12:3 (NIV)

Jesus didn't seek to be understood. After His resurrection, He didn't try to explain to people how hard it was to carry the weight of everyone's sins on His shoulders. His example is something I try to understand, but I can't fully. I can't understand giving your life freely to people who curse your name, betray you, don't believe you, and treat you like trash.

Jesus was an intricately intentional, compassionate, wounded healer. I repeat those three words: Intentional. Compassionate. Wounded. As He spat in the mud and placed it on a man's eyes so the man could see again, as He tirelessly inconvenienced himself to travel across seas and long distances to bring healing to just one or thousands of souls, as he loved the little children, as he wept, as he showed unmerited compassion, Jesus modeled for us how to handle hardships and how to rely on the Father during them. He came into our world, he lived among us, and he loved us. He uniquely addressed people's situations on a case-to-case basis, and he left the 99 for the one.

He told a man that his sins were forgiven after the man's friends had carried him on a mat to Jesus, then told that man to pick up his mat and walk after proving to the teachers of the law that he had authority on earth to forgive sins. He was intentional. He was compassionate. He had pain and yet was healing those around him. He modeled for us what it is to be a wounded healer.

Jesus also modeled for us what it means to humble yourself and be quiet even when every fiber in you wants to seek your own justice and vindication. When he was beaten, Jesus was silent. When Pilate questioned him, He was silent. When He stood before his people next to Barnabas, He was silent. And after seven short sentences, He silently died there on that tree. Jesus didn't seek out what he rightfully deserved; He only sought to obey His Father.

Job and Joseph

As I began to grow more empathy for hurting people, I began to sense that there was something much deeper happening under the surface and that God was giving me an opportunity to speak into some people's lives, not despite but *because* of what I had been through. If I had not faced those moments that could've been faith-shattering, I wouldn't have had the opportunity to learn about the love and compassion that every one of us broken vessels is desperately longing for. Those moments caused me to settle deeper into my faith. Those moments gave me more understanding for people that many would call "losers" or "crazy people." As I began to dive into the story of Job repeatedly, I was slowly seeing a little more of God's character.

To see sick people not get well can be so discouraging. It can be infuriating to yearn for God's kingdom here on earth and not see it. I believe that Jesus has full authority to tear down strongholds, bondages, disease, you name it. We have access to that same authority through Jesus. So that means that sickness, depression, and satan himself must bow down to the name of Jesus. I believe that it all does.

'The Lord said to Satan, "Very well, then, everything he has is in your power, but on the man himself do not lay a finger." Then Satan went out from the presence of the Lord.' -Job 1:12 (NIV)

But what about Job? What was God revealing through Job? Why was God delaying Job's vindication? Have there been moments since Job between the Lord and satan where the Lord says again about another one of his faithful servants, "you can have everything, just don't take their life"? Has God had conversations with satan about particular people and given him permission to take ground, knowing that they would remain faithful to the Father no matter what?

I have no idea. It's just a thought that I think is worth provoking in our minds before assuming that so-and-so hasn't prayed hard enough, worked hard enough, or is living in sin, and that's why they're suffering. There are constant moments happening in the unseen realm that is just as real as our world and has been around thousands of years longer than you and I have.

When I read through the book of Job, I see a unique and complex picture that I didn't allow my mind to explore before. I see someone who stayed faithful to God in his suffering, and yet the enemy continued to have access to Job. That is, until the day God said no more.

It's so important to remember that it isn't even a fight between God and satan. The moment even the smallest sliver of a pigment of God's glorious light shines, darkness automatically flees. Satan wants us to fear him. Many churches feed into this and don't talk about satan's tactics and if they do, they do it in a way that instills fear. We gain freedom when we reach a point where we're no longer afraid of him or his tactics.

At the end of it all, God rebukes Job and tells him to pray for His friends who have wrongly accused him, and finally, there is God's vindication after such horrible tragedies. Yet even then, with so much restored, there are still questions. So many things that Job went through seemed unnecessary. He had new children, but he never received the ones that died.

The story of Job shows me my need for God. It shows me that God rebukes me for my good. It shows that there are things here on earth that we'll never understand. It shows that things happen in the spiritual realm that we can't understand. The friends who had nothing good to say to Job reveal that if we don't truly tune into how God wants us to see things and hear His voice, our mouths can become weapons and no longer instruments of God to the hurting people around us.

As humans, our instincts are to look to someone or something to blame when we don't understand suffering. Or we may judge people because we don't understand their behaviors. Or we may try to control the suffering, or we may just be in denial and act like what people are going through isn't real.

After years of beating myself up about having a disease that was never my fault in the first place, I've come to learn firsthand that not all of what we face is in our control. I don't think that God gave our friend cancer in order that they learn a lesson. Yes, maybe cancer has taught our friend some things, but I do not believe that God threw that on them, or that our friend's daily suffering is their fault. Sadly, we look for someone to blame, but sometimes ailments come simply to bring glory to God.

About eight years ago, a friend sent me a video about a pastor named Bob Sorge. Bob had a great deal of things taken away from him, including an accident many years ago that gave him an obscure medical condition that made it painful for him to even speak. As a worship leader and pastor at the time, I imagine he felt useless.

Bob said something at the beginning of the video that I will never forget. He said, "God could have left Job alone." That one line changed me. No matter what others said about Job, it didn't matter in the end. Jesus promised to be with us to the very end of the age, so as we suffer, we can rest assured. The sweetest fragrance that comes from a rose is when it is crushed.

And then, there was Joseph. Humble, compassionate, wise, spirit-filled Joseph. A man of integrity and character. A man with a gift from God that was stewarded, even in the fires.

The story of Joseph is one of my favorite stories in the bible of all time. It's a story of faithfulness, redemption, and promotion through pain. It's a story about a boy who had a dream from God and instead of seeing that dream come to fruition as he stepped into adulthood, he went through over a decade of detours, humiliation, slavery, false accusations, and basically everything else that felt opposite of what a good God would allow in his life.

But Joseph grew in the fires. And the Lord brought about Joseph's promotion only after many years of isolation, pain, and betrayal. 13 years to be exact. Joseph was seventeen years old when his brothers sold him into slavery. He wasn't fully released from captivity until he was thirty.

"So Pharaoh asked them, 'Can we find anyone like this man, one in whom is the spirit of God?' Then Pharaoh said to Joseph, 'Since God has made all this known to you, there is no one so discerning and wise as you. You shall be in charge of my palace, and all my people are to submit to your orders. Only with respect to the throne will I be greater than you.' So Pharaoh said to Joseph, 'I hereby put you in charge of the whole land of Egypt.' Then Pharaoh took his signet ring from his finger and put it on Joseph's finger. He dressed him in robes of fine linen and put a gold chain around his neck. He had him ride in a chariot as

his second-in command, and people shouted before him,
'Make way!' Thus he put him in charge of the whole land
of Egypt." - Genesis 41: 38 - 43 (NIV)

Finally: *vindication.* As he rode in a chariot bedazzled in
honor and authority, as the second most powerful man in
Egypt, Joseph remained humble. Joseph went on to do
many great things and devoted himself to the good of others
for the rest of his life.

It's astounding that after he was released from prison,
Joseph chose to extend mercy, compassion, forgiveness,
and grace towards the ones who were the whole reason he
was ever thrown into slavery in the first place. Joseph's heart
was still soft after all those years.

"Joseph said to his brothers, 'I am Joseph! Is my father still
living?' But his brothers were not able to answer him,
because they were terrified at his presence. Then Joseph
said to his brothers, 'Come close to me.' When they had
done so, he said, 'I am your brother Joseph, the one you
sold into Egypt! And now, do not be distressed and do not
be angry with yourselves for selling me here, because it was
to save lives that God sent me ahead of you. For two years
now there has been famine in the land, and for the next
five years there will be no plowing and reaping. But God
sent me ahead of you to preserve for you a remnant on
earth and to save your lives by a great deliverance. 'So
then, it was not you who sent me here, but God. He made
me father to Pharaoh, lord of his entire household and
ruler of all Egypt. Now hurry back to my father and say to
him, 'This is what your son Joseph says: God has made me
lord of all Egypt. Come down to me; don't delay. You shall
live in the region of Goshen and be near me—you, your
children and grandchildren, your flocks and herds, and all
you have. I will provide for you there, because five years of
famine are still to come. Otherwise, you and your
household and all who belong to you will become

destitute' -Genesis 45: 3–11 (NIV)

As if all of that wasn't enough, Joseph then supplied the ones who had betrayed him with wagons, new garments, silver money, and twenty additional donkeys carrying provisions for the journey.

Something Deeper, Something Better

Sometimes God is doing something entirely beneath the surface of our lives. In the secret place, in the silence, and the loneliest of seasons away from all the hustle and bustle. We may look around during these seasons, and all we see is our lack, unfinished work and the disappointment that our lives may feel like. It's not a disappointment, though. Something of greater value has been taking place in our souls. Sanctification. Pruning. Bringing our lives through a funnel until what remains is the rich, everlasting stuff that legitimately matters.

Pain can birth in anyone not only more sympathy but real *empathy*. Lyme disease forced me to stop sheepishly wondering how to pray for someone who was hurting because now, after sharing in suffering with Jesus, my prayer life had changed. I could relate on a level that most people my age couldn't. I could sit with hurting people without trying to find an explanation, something or someone to blame, or trying to fix their problems. The truth is that people who are deeply hurting or grieving often do not even need any words but rather the gentle comfort of a silent soul sitting there next to them.

That soul acknowledges that although they don't understand the silent suffering their friend is facing, they're there for them.

What Hurting People Yearn For

Prayer is not a formula or a magic power, nor should it be controlled or theologized. It comes flowing out of a thankful heart. What if when we prayed for people, we refrained from praying, "if you want to heal him or her", and instead solely prayed with the faith that God gives us? My honest struggle when praying for others is in allowing my expectations and fleshly thoughts to fall at the feet of Jesus and to not get in the way of what He wants to do. I still believe that His heart is always to heal. He weeps over every broken body in this world. The healing we are waiting for may simply not look like anything anyone expects. It may come in the form of someone living in a wheelchair for the rest of their life, but their soul being healed and God using them for his kingdom.

What if we no longer said, "Lord, if there's something they need to learn before you heal them "... again, we prayed with the faith that God has given us. I don't see fruit in praying such things. Why say something that condemns or confuses someone who is already suffering? I have learned that God is the only One who knows their heart - I don't. I don't always need to open my mouth. Sometimes there are holy matters between people and God, and it should stay that way.

What we believe about God affects the people around us. If we believe that He is a stern God who gives us hardships in order that we learn a lesson, we're missing it. If we think that God won't give us more than we can handle even though that verse is regarding temptation ("no temptation has overtaken you except what is common to mankind. And God is faithful, He will not let you be tempted beyond what you can bear. But when you are tempted, He will also provide a way out so you can endure it" – 1 Corinthians 10:13), again: we're missing it. Paul is addressing sin, not suffering.

God has allowed me to endure more than I can handle every day. He also gives me grace. He gives me strength. He sustains me. And when I come to the end of myself the next day, there He is supplying me with what I need again.

I've had multiple people at church services pray for me

and push on my chest with force while praying for me. God doesn't do that. It's very unpeaceful when you're being prayed over by someone unaware of this, and it makes me want to stop reaching out for prayer from church leaders.

As I reflect on my journey, I can say that the piercing judgments in the eyes of Christians have happened regularly over the last decade. I've felt burned many times that I've chosen to open up. Can I just say that we, as Christians, can be some of the most judgmental clad of people ever? Criticism and unbelief over your suffering from people you thought were safe and accepted you can make you feel hurt, unsafe, and frankly not want to be around them.

The judgments and criticism that we Christians carry towards others can truly affect how people perceive Jesus, especially people who are not yet mature in their faith. Thankfully, Jesus has been gracious with me after all the hurtful moments I've experienced in the church and continues to be. He's given me the courage to forgive. He's mended my heart, and He's given me grace and understanding for people who have hurt me.

You may have been to a church that was a poor representation of God, but that's not on Him. The truth is that the bridegroom has a fierce and jealous love for his bride, the church, which is full of imperfect people like me because we live in an imperfect and sinful world.

The church is still meant to be a refuge for hurting people. Imagine every church across America not only open on Sundays but every day of the week for people who need somewhere to sleep. Imagine grand churches with their elaborate and "hip" designs using the money they'd be spending on the style of their churches to instead open their doors to homeless people every night to give them food and shelter. What if the church wasn't the "social club" that so many people view it as this day in age? I think the western church would reach many more hurting people who need the church.

I've had the privilege to be a part of many church

families around the world that showed the love of God in their actions by truly serving the "least of these," and my community now has its fair share of genuinely compassionate people. I only share this to shed light on what some of the chronically ill, the outcasts, and many other groups of people may feel in the church when we, as Christians, decide to judge instead of love. Maybe it can even allow us to open our eyes and our hearts a little more to those who are silently suffering around us.

God Can Still Be Trusted

Whether it's a scary diagnosis, loss of a loved one, a broken family, so much debt it keeps you up at night, a job loss, divorce, abuse, not even wanting to live - I know, I've been there. It can all be so heavy.

There is still hope, grace, and might I add absolute joy that's available to you and me, even now. Jesus is hope. When we're stuck in our heads, grace says, "I love you. You are fearfully and wonderfully made. I've never been prouder of you." Jesus gives joy - a contagious childlike joy that is only found in His presence. "The joy of the Lord is your strength" (from Nehemiah 8:10 NIV).

People will fail us, and we will fail them too. We will feel misunderstood. I heard Lauren Daigle once say that true freedom is giving others permission to misunderstand you.

Though it may not seem like it, there's still good out there. There's still good in here, in our hearts, and in our homes. In people. In you. In me. I see the good because I'd be foolish not to by now. In my home. In my body. In my community. In my marriage.

I know there is good when I see grace in the eyes of my husband. I know there is good by the way God provides for me. By the fact that I get to wake up every morning and breathe.

I've got to believe that this healing millions of us are waiting for... it's for a greater purpose, and that the masterpiece that God is painting through our lives is so much grander than what we can see. This isn't mindless suffering. It may take a while to get to the other side, but we will get there - eventually.

Our lives may look and feel like chaotic messes, but in the minuscule moments, in the calming down of our hearts and souls to hear His voice, even in our anger and moments of doubt, there's a deepening in the richness of the soil of our souls. As we get our hands in the mud and get a closer look at our soil, we see the cultivation that has taken place. We see new sprouts. As we look up, we realize there's a garden that's been growing out of our souls this whole time, and it's only getting more vibrant and unique as time goes on.

Our processes of getting from point a to point b may not look or feel good the slightest bit, but we will come out on the other side stronger, more radiant, and with more compassion.

You may be looking for more conclusions or answers as to why some people must go through a gamut of trials, why Job went through what he did, or why you've gone through the tragedies that you've gone through. I want to give you all the answers, and I want something or someone to blame, but it doesn't do me any good.

Raising my gaze to the only One who can heal me is how I get through the day. I don't always feel Him, but beneath the surface of every semblance, beneath all the rubbish - there He is, standing in the doorway with His arms wide open. There's so much to discover about our Savior.

After we breathe that very last breath, we will enter paradise. We will marvel in reverence every day as we see God and a surfeit of spectacular creations in Heaven that He's kept private from the public. Everything will be entirely different, and every part of us will be fully restored: including our bodies.

To forgive those who have wronged us is a key to our own healing, even if that healing hasn't happened in our bodies yet. Our souls and hearts can be healed while our bodies are waiting. The forgiveness we extend speaks volumes to those who know they have wronged you and me. We may not trust them anymore, which is perfectly fine, but we must forgive. "But if you do not forgive others their sins, your Father will not forgive your sins" (Matthew 6:15 NIV).

God can still be trusted. It may not be believable to you yet, but the truth is that He is the most trustworthy being ever. Even when we are doubting to believe, to be able to muster up the words, "I don't understand, but I trust you God," is a powerful act. And I assure you that in due time, sometimes in the most unexpected of ways, He promotes His servants.

CHAPTER SEVEN
23 ½

"It is good to wait quietly for the salvation of the Lord. It is good for a man to bear the yoke while he is young. Let him sit alone in silence, for the Lord has laid it on him. Let him bury his face in the dust - there may yet be hope. Let him offer his cheek to one who would strike him and let him be filled with disgrace.
For no one is cast off by the Lord forever.
Though he brings grief, he will show compassion,
So great is his unfailing love. For He does not willingly bring affliction or grief to anyone."
Lamentations 3: 26-33 (NIV)

It was a cold and dreary morning. As I saw 3:30 a.m. plastered across the clock that gave a small sliver of light into my pitch-black room, I tossed and turned only to come to the realization that I probably wasn't going to fall back asleep because of the pain I was in. A couple weeks had passed since my trip to Cali, and God had done so much in my heart, but I struggled to know how to move forward in a positive direction with my health anymore.

Like it was Groundhog Day, I got dressed and dragged

my body down the stairs and into the kitchen. I pondered there silently alone in that quiet kitchen with the bright lights on while it was still dark outside. I'd soon be sitting in an airplane overlooking a slice of Washington's beauty, settling into my window seat, thanking God for that season and for all the marvelous souls that had walked into my life. A few hours after that, I'd be in the Nashville airport, finally hugging my mom who I hadn't seen in a long time.

That morning I felt burning pain and chaos inside my body, and yet, simultaneously, I was at peace. I felt complete. The last six months of my life had been full of days I didn't want to relive. My naturopath was confident that I would heal quickly after the dental procedure I had done six months prior and that other health issues would resolve themselves with the treatments I was doing after the procedure. So, I was naturally disappointed when I was still in bad shape six months later - a letdown followed by a whirlwind of other letdowns.

My time in Seattle had been full of internal growth that will stick with me for the rest of my life - constant moments of being stretched so thin I thought I'd break, but God held me together. At the end of the day, I knew that all my health practitioners had given their best shot to help me heal. I had to extend more grace to people and remember that God is my ultimate healer, that His power is incomparable, and that He is faithful to fulfill His promises. I was reminded that my healing is on God's shoulders, not the shoulders of man.

I took a hard look at my life there and then at 23 ½ years old, all the random things that I'd done, all the stories. All the pain, all the blessings lavished on me in pain. I quietly muttered, "Lord, it is painful to obey your voice at times."

As my life flashed before my eyes, I heard a voice that was not the voice of my Father say, "there is nothing to show for any of it. You've got nothing Lauren," and I remembered how in the eyes of the world, that was pretty accurate. I didn't go to school or get a degree, I had no life savings, I wasn't married, I didn't have a car, and I hadn't had my own home in years. Life had been full of suffering, and what was there to even show for it?

Countless experiences that changed me to my core and put more love in my heart. Countless moments where I was taught how to dance upon disappointment. More meaning, purpose, and people that I adore. That was all God's doing in my life. And so, I concluded that the voice that was telling me I had nothing is the voice of a coward. Truth is, the enemy who thinks he rules over our world has it all backwards.

As followers of Jesus, we get to have life. We get to have joy. We are co-heirs with Christ. We get to have an intimate relationship with the God of the universe.

Don't hear me wrong: being a follower of Jesus doesn't mean things will be easier by any means. Walking out disease with Jesus doesn't mean that it's always going to make sense. Sometimes He has led me to places where I get sicker, and I have to rely on Him more. Sometimes I have to rely on people around me more in the process too, and it's a complete breakdown of my pride - which is necessary.

So, why do I continue to follow Him even when it would be easier not to? In short, because He's worthy. Because He's working everything out for my good. Because, in the end, I know that life will pan out a trillion times better when I've trusted Him. Because of the promise of eternal life free of pain and every other terrible thing in this world.

Chronic illness can feel embarrassing at times. My situation probably didn't need to feel so shameful, but because I was stuck in lies, I felt embarrassed about lyme most of the time. I felt like too much. Asking someone to open a jar for you or drive you somewhere can feel humiliating. It feels embarrassing having to back out of things I've committed to by telling my friends yet again that I'm "not feeling well" because I'm tired of being blatantly honest about how bad I feel, and most people are tired of hearing it. God's still not tired of hearing it.

Outrageous Love

Staring out from my little window seat that morning past the wing of the plane and through the clouds, was an endless sublime of snow capped mountain ranges as far as my eyes could see. I was reminded there in that seat of how deep, how wide, and how high God's furious love is, and how close He truly was. I don't know how you can look at nature and all its breath-taking treasures and still not believe in the one who created all of nature, humanity, time, energy, love, and everything else, for that matter.

Those past seven months in Seattle had been full of challenging twists and turns that were met with wild depth and grace. Sitting on my doctor's table, realizing that even with tremendous resources and great wisdom, we as humans are still so limited.

After doing the things that I'd felt the Lord leading me to do and still experiencing many if not more physical limitations, what I knew and held onto was that God was with me, and He was for me. "You Yourself have recorded my wanderings. Put my tears in Your bottle. Are they not in Your records? Then my enemies will retreat on the day when I call. This I know: God is for me" - Psalm 56: 8-9 (HCSB).

When I moved back to Tennessee, I felt jaded towards doctors and the medical community as a whole. The dental implants that I got in Germany had fallen out, Nischwitz's office was asking for more money for the surgery after I had paid them all I thought they had asked for, and I was frustrated. After all the medical treatment I had received, the specialists who worked with me had more money in their pockets, but I was still sick. I didn't want to see any more doctors or specialists.

Then I heard through the grapevine of a Christian lyme disease specialist in Tennessee named Tamara. She offered me a free phone consultation where I believe the Holy Spirit gave her insight into my situation. The first time I came into Tamara's clinic, she washed my feet and prayed healing over my body. Never have I met any other health practitioner who invited Jesus into their medical practice the way she does.

God used Tamara to bring me hope again. I believe He used her to not only bring me more healing and hope, but to save my life. After performing in-depth testing, she sat down and cried with me, exclaiming how she didn't know how I was still alive. She then did everything she could to help me get my life back.

I spent many days lying on the beds there at that clinic, but as the days and weeks went on, I was getting positive results through Tamara's completely new therapeutic approaches. I found myself bursting with life and invigorated with inspiration. I was highly hopeful, which was scary.

It's scary to keep carrying hope for something you've longed for most of your life. It's scary knowing that chronic illness could come knocking on the door of your body tomorrow morning, even louder than it did yesterday or a year ago. It's scary knowing that you could look like a fool when you lose another job because you couldn't keep up with its demands, another relationship, or another dream.

But why should I care what people think? Why should I be scared? Why should I stop dreaming? I love the life that I've been given. Exploring, painting, sitting with people dissimilar from myself, looking into their eyes, being still before God, being connected. Loving the woman that God has created me to be. Loving who is in front of me. Loving, Loving, loving. The human heart beats on this one thing.

I used to be scared. Scared of myself, scared of what I'd find in the murky depths of my soul. Scared of chasing my dreams. Scared of turning around and praying for the lady that I just walked by on the street. Scared of what I want, scared of my emotions. Scared of opening my heart. What I have found is that there is nothing to fear. The love of God hits my fears in the gut. The love of God destroys the enemy's grip.

At 23 ½ years old, I had been beaten down but not destroyed; no, I was stronger than before because I knew that every ounce of my strength came from above. It was then that I concluded something basic yet monumental: God loves me. God loves you. We are not only loved, we are cherished by our all-powerful Father. I want to keep going back to this again and again and again, for the rest of my life, like a little kid who keeps coming back to her dad's lap.

The Lord Almighty is personal with you and me. He loves every aching, bleeding part of our hearts just as much as the whole, healthy parts. You are adored just the way you are. No makeup, no smile, no perfect 10-year plan. And if people don't like you for who you are, that's a shame because you are a masterpiece.

Blatant honesty, vulnerability, and love are things that this world is thirsting for. I see it in people's eyes every day. We all need the hands of Jesus to intimately grasp our own. We need His love more than anything.

We can all get lost at sea from time to time, and we all need him to carry us back to shore every time. So, let's extend our hands to Him like we mean it, like we *are* lost at sea, like we can't go on without Him, like we literally trust Him with our lives, and are expectant to watch Him calm our storms and do the impossible. He will do it.

Jesus was in the stern, sleeping on a cushion. The disciples woke him and said to him, "Teacher, don't you care if we drown?" He got up, rebuked the wind and said to the waves, "Quiet! Be still!" Then the wind died down and it was completely calm. He said to his disciples, "Why are you so afraid? Do you still have no faith?"
Mark 4:38-40 (NIV)

Resting Like Koalas

I love the story of Jesus sleeping inside the boat while everyone else is panicking. Jesus sleeping in the boat in the middle of a windstorm signals that he's not worried. He knows he isn't going to die. He knows that His Father is going to take care of him.

After rebuking the wind, Jesus asked his disciples, "why are you afraid? Have you still no faith?" Jesus knew that we as humans are prone to fear and faithlessness. He knew that satan's desire is to make us fearful and faithless until we are unable to hear the voice of God anymore.

I thoroughly enjoy my life more when I'm well-rested. I'm less scatter-brained. More relaxed. More gentle and caring. More intentional about where I place my energy.

This is tapping into the good stuff. I know that I'm not Superwoman anymore who can conquer any and every assignment on my own. I know that I'm not supposed to be in control of everything. Although it can take a lot of surrender to get here, I thrive from this place.

This place is somewhere away from the city, traffic, sirens, alarms, neighbor's music, and all the other obnoxious noises that raise our heart rates and blood pressure. This place is a quiet place with fresh air and a clear mind, seeing what lies ahead through a new lens as you hear the birds chirping again. There's profound peace and clarity here.

Sabbath is not about being bored, it's about letting go of everything and being free in the arms of our Maker. It's about saying, "I cannot sustain my body, my finances, my relationships, my time, or my life without you. You and You alone sustain me, so here I am submitting myself to You again today."

There was a time in my life where I had no literal concept of the rest of God. I had no idea what it meant to "operate out of rest." In the midst of waking up before 5 a.m. to take a bumpy road uphill to an orphanage to go cook another breakfast, going to the border and feeding the homeless, hosting house builds, asking my leader what she wanted me to do next, being in the prayer house all night, eating anything that said "cheap" and "fast" so that I could get back to "ministry," I thought that I was doing good things. And sure, what I was doing were all works that society says are "good." But rest was a foreign concept to me in all my running around and serving so much that eventually led to complete depletion.

I think that can be a danger zone: doing "good" things and being a "good" Christian. What even is a "good" Christian? "Why do you call me good?" Jesus answered. "No one is good—except God alone" - Luke 18:19 (NIV). Relationship is what transforms, not "good" behavior or doing good things for God.

In all of the going, going, going, the noise, the poor sleep habits - I hadn't given myself any room to sincerely rest. I had little to no understanding of all that Sabbath represents. I took it lightly that it's a command (one of the Ten Commandments to be accurate) and why it was and is so important.

God made the Sabbath for us, and He commanded that we practice it every week. He knew how prone we are to wander, beat ourselves up, push ourselves beyond our limits, and put off rest in order to gain more sense of control. He knew how prone we are to keep brushing off those hobbies that we've yearned to put our hands to instead of hiding them under the rug.

We continue to run around doing a bunch of tasks and duties for the church or the ministry, and we forget about that part where we let go, and we rest. The part where He begins restoring our souls again and brings us back to life. We forget to pick up that hobby we've been putting off for ages. We forget to look at our spouses and enjoy the marriage that's right in front of us or the friendships right in front of us. We forget how to live.

Paul encourages us to "make every effort to enter into rest" (Hebrews 4:11 NIV). Another translation says, "strive to enter into his rest" (ESV version). It takes effort and intention to rest. That's why we see satan making so many people busybodies. If he can't make you sin or believe lies, he'll make you so busy you won't be able to hear God anymore.

Maybe there's more to this whole rest thing. Maybe I need to live at a slower pace. Resting is not quitting. Resting is surrendering and trusting. Rest breeds more contentment and satisfaction.

Maybe nurturing my soul and tapping into the stillness that's right here in front of me will allow me to hear my Father's voice again. Maybe my body's naturally doing what it knows it needs to do today, ironically on the Sabbath: rest.

One animal who is all about that slow life is the koala. Koalas sleep on average 20 hours a day, and at most, 22 hours. They're basically resting all the time. As they hang out at home, a sturdy tree branch, they keep things simple by eating one plant that nearly nobody else can eat - eucalyptus. Eucalyptus is full of toxins that would kill you and me if we had even a tiny amount, and yet the way God has designed koalas has given them the ability to tolerate those toxins.

People don't feel threatened by them, nor are koalas threatened by other animals. Koalas are sitting high above all the madness. They sit in a position that would be uncomfortable to be in 24/7, yet God has given them a special something to make it more bearable for them to sit: they have cartilage by the end of their spine and extra fur on their bums which provides more padding.

Koalas remind me that when we allow Jesus to be the complete sustainer of our life, no weapon can stand against us. They remind me to go sit in the Heavenly places with my King. When I remember that I have a seat in Heaven, that there's a place prepared for me there, how can I not rest in Him and trust Him?

And just like God gives the koala a special something on their bum to help with the discomfort, God will grant me what I need as I continue to sit in my aches with Him. God cares for the koalas and accommodates their weaknesses, not based on anything they're doing, but because He's a loving Creator. How much more will he care for us and accommodate our all weaknesses?

"Look at the birds of the air; they do not sow or reap or
store away in barns, and yet your heavenly Father feeds
them. Are you not much more valuable than they? Can any
one of you by worrying add a single hour to your life?
"And why do you worry about clothes? See how the
flowers of the field grow. They do not labor or spin. Yet I
tell you that not even Solomon in all his splendor was
dressed like one of these. If that is how God clothes the
grass of the field, which is here today and tomorrow is
thrown into the fire, will he not much more clothe you -
you of little faith?" - Matthew 6: 26-30 (NIV)

In life, we have thousands of things to try to fill
ourselves with. Money, attention, food – things we indulge
in to try to satisfy our souls. But koalas take the one thing
they need, it fills them up, and they're filled with rest. This
reminds me that if I stop trying to substitute all the things I
try to fill my voids with and instead just go to the bread of
life, God will give me rest. He will put my enemies under
my feet.

Never Alone
We all have a story to tell, and we've all experienced
some sort of pain, whether it's silent or loud. I meet rich
people who seem to have it all, and yet their hearts are
hurting beyond words. The only constant, 100% reliable
and stable, most intimate relationship available to us is with
Jesus.

I once was sitting on a dried-up log on a beach in
Edmonds, Washington, with my new friend, Steve. Steve
drove a blue van with one of those white stick-figure family
stickers on the back with two cats and a dog. He named the
van Moses because Moses got him to his own promised
land, which was Seattle at the time. Steve's mom passed
away when he was five.

As I quietly stared at God's creation in front of me, a massive mountain range that took my breath away, Steve asked me what the most beautiful place I had ever been to was. I answered swiftly and confidently with, "La Comarca" - a breath-taking region in Panama. After I answered, though, I had flashbacks of other places and experiences over the years that have shaped me, and I wondered if I had answered the question too quickly.

I asked Steve the same question, and he wasn't as sure. He mentioned Israel, the sea of Galilee, and an experience he had where he knew that he was sitting on the same beach where Jesus had cooked breakfast for his disciples. Then, as he proceeded to ponder on various experiences, he began to talk about the locations he had more recently been to. He said that those places were marked by something different than the experiences in high school or early years of college.

Those places were strung on a line of not necessarily where he was, but more so the fact that only God was with him in all those experiences. They were no longer experiences he could reminisce over with friends, because there was no physical person with him on the 150 miles of hiking he had embarked on that summer or the sunsets he spent alone on the beach with Jesus. Steve had come to the realization that he was never alone. No human needed to validate that for him.

It's quite remarkable the things that we do when we know that we aren't alone. When I remember that I'm not alone, I make bolder decisions. I care less about what people think. I stop being swayed by the opinions of others more than what God says.

Unquestionably, there is profound wisdom in seeking counsel, being surrounded by community, having mentors – all are important, and I do not undermine those things. I glean from all those voices in my own life. But those voices aren't God's voice.

At the heart of it, I think we're all afraid much of the time. Afraid of being vulnerable, afraid of losing our reputations. Afraid of change. We forget who our ultimate friend, counselor, mentor, and Savior is. We forget how powerful He is and what He is capable of when we are holding hands with Him.

I wonder what life would be like if you and I began visualizing Jesus there with us in everything. Not just in the scary moments, but in the dull, ordinary days that don't seem to amount to anything. The days the rain hits our sidewalks, and our cloudy minds get lost in the tasks scribbled on the to-do lists of our fridges. The days that sneak away from us.

What if we envisioned Jesus lying in bed with us when we fell asleep and when we woke up, and what if we started to truly believe that He is with us... always? Would our trust and faith grow incrementally stronger? Would we be tasting His goodness more? Would we trust Him more?

If imagining the Lord next to you makes you feel uncomfortable, I get it. I can't tell you how many times I have pushed him away because it feels too scary and hard. He remains patient.

There is no one like our God. What other God sends the Holy Spirit, angels, and tangible reminders of His love to people to remind them how much He loves them? What other God sends His son to die for sinful and selfish people like us? He is the one and only true God. He is after our hearts, and He doesn't give up on us even when it feels like everyone else does.

So, the question is, do we want his closeness? I'm asking myself this question because acknowledging Jesus and giving Him all my trust requires a kind of surrender that I don't necessarily enjoy. It requires a deep awareness that God is there and a realization that his might is always so much grander than anything I can muster up from myself.

It may not seem like it, and it may not be easy by any means to trust Him again, but I assure you that He is here, and He is ready to walk beside you - whatever your life looks like today.

CHAPTER EIGHT

Letting Go

"They have greatly oppressed me from my youth,
Let Israel say, "they have greatly oppressed me from my
youth, but they have not gained the victory over me.
Plowmen have plowed my back and made their furrows
long. But the Lord is righteous; He has cut me free from
the cords of the wicked. May all who hate Zion be turned
back in shame."
Psalm 129: 1-5 (NIV)

Sometimes our bodies are stuck in trauma. Sometimes
there are scars that leave such a mark on us that we live our
lives differently because of them. Maybe we had an abuser
that broke us down so severely that we don't even know
how to find ourselves anymore underneath all the pain.
Maybe we decide that we won't let anyone in anymore, or
we'll never put ourselves in a certain kind of situation again.
We're afraid and we're holding on for dear life, waiting for
something to change but we don't know how it ever will
change. Healing from trauma can feel tricky and never-
ending at times, but the rewards that come with it are
priceless.

"Thanks for coming," he said in a sarcastic tone as he natulantly walked out of the hotel lobby. As he made his way out the front door, he threw a peace sign up in the air, not even making eye contact with my sister Becca and me - or saying goodbye for that matter. Becca and I proceeded to book our hotel room there in New Mexico. We hadn't been safe with our dad as kids, and we realized yet again that we still weren't safe with him as adults. Becca and I had believed that time was going to be a restorative and healing time spending Thanksgiving with our dad, who lived in New Mexico, but that's the last thing this was.

After another night of scaring his now adult daughters, my dad had successfully convinced us to leave our Thanksgiving with him and his wife early. Maybe you can relate with me that when you have a parent that acts like a child, you learn to roll with the punches. I didn't know that day in that random hotel that I wouldn't see my dad for the next eight years - and counting - or that in five years, I would stop talking to him altogether.

It's astounding how the word father has the ability to bring up such a variety of emotions for people. No matter what age or level of maturity, relationships with our earthly fathers inevitably affect us. For some, they experience joy when they think of the word because their dad is the best man that they know. For others, there is a depth of grief because they lost their father. For others, there is sadness or anger or disappointment over the abandonment of their father, and for others, there are not the right words or emotions that can describe what the word "father" means to them.

Fathers play such a vital role in their kids' lives. The way a father loves his family has a massive influence on them. They can represent Jesus or be unsafe and unloving, both having very positive and negative ripple effects on the family. The influence that the father has is monumental in cultivating the culture of the family and the home.

I still don't have the right words to describe everything

that I've walked through with my earthly father or how the scars he left me inevitably affect me. After walking through forgiveness, I began to internally put pressure on myself to continue to have a relationship with my dad. I wanted to show him the heart of Jesus, yet I didn't consider his lack of efforts, how toxic the relationship was to me, or how he had threatened me along with other family members time and time again. I wanted to make the relationship work so desperately that I was too blind to see what was toxic.

Sooner or later, I began to realize patterns in myself. I could go months without talking to my dad, and my health would slowly be improving. Yet the moment that he decided to say another demeaning thing to me, I would fall into the same shame and guilt spirals again. I'd beat myself up as the wounding words of my dad echoed in my mind. So, I set some more serious boundaries that have been in place for years, and I'm much better because of it. My marriage is much better because of it.

No man is going to love God's precious daughters the way that our ultimate Father does. Maybe you've heard it before but don't believe it, or it just sounds cliche, but it's true. No matter where we come from or how loved or unloved that we felt as kids, there's an incomparable love to be found in our Father's arms.

I don't know what the word father means to you. I don't know how it feels when you think of God as your ultimate Father. What I do know is that He is not finished with you, dear one. What you try to hide or forget, He brings to the light and brings dignity where there was never supposed to be shame. He writes new stories over our lives that we could've never imagined. He says, "come and drink and receive my daughter. My son. Taste and see that I am good. Always have been, always will be."

It's Okay to Not Be Okay

Maybe you had an unloving parent, too. Maybe like me, your heart is in the process of mending from the wounds

107

that you've had a hard time saying out loud over the years. And yet, putting words to those wounds and expressing our emotions over those wounds can be a tool to open the door for more healing. This is because you're no longer in denial.

If you have chronic illness, I'm sure you can relate to the wedges in relationships that can happen due to your illness. That's what happened in my relationship with my mom. I believe that the enemy began to use lyme to destroy my mom and I's relationship, which only seemed to fall apart more as time went on.

I've learned in life that the only one who won't let me down is Jesus. He hasn't abandoned or rejected me. He's been healing the broken parts of me. I don't minimize the emotional pain I've experienced anymore; I'm feeling it and grieving it. I'm not giving myself a timeline for things to be "okay" in certain relationships. It's okay for things to not be okay. It's okay to express the anger that's been suppressed. It's okay to release what always needed to be released.

As I age, mend, and eventually flourish and thrive, I look forward to the days that I'll have more energy for certain relationships. I trust that God will salvage whatever is salvageable. But for now, I'm simply giving myself the grace to mend and heal from the pain. I'm letting go.

I believe that many of us can't let go and fully release whatever needs to be released. We're worried about what might happen. We're worried that we'll hurt the people who hurt us, even though we're not responsible for how people respond to the positive choices we've made in order to become emotionally healthier.

I believe we've also made vows in our hearts that because the people who hurt us the most are family that we can't set certain boundaries with them. And yet, setting those boundaries can help our hearts mend, other relationships flourish, and our physical health can improve exponentially. Setting those boundaries help the people who have hurt us, too. Expecting good things to come out of a toxic relationship isn't fair to you or the other person you're trying to have a relationship with.

There's more in store for our lives than what we can imagine. There's more energy to be tapped into. All the energy we once spent on trying to survive or making the wrong relationships work can now be spent on our passions. We do not have to say yes to relationships that aren't good for our souls. We do not have to put pressure on ourselves in our relationships to be what we can't be.

Making yourself less available to toxic relationships does not mean that you are bitter. I believe it can save you from bitterness at times because you're drawing lines of the sand of how much you can take, which teaches people how to treat you.

Letting go means surrender to me. Letting go is about releasing my hands and giving up whatever is not doing me any good anymore so I can pick up the better thing. Sometimes it's a thought pattern, a dream, or a relationship that I need to release. What I'm holding onto so tightly is no longer healthy, life-giving, or fruitful. There's no place for it in my life anymore.

Letting go is about shedding years of guilt, shame, and pain. Letting go means forgiving and moving forward as my whole self, not leaving any part of me behind. Letting go is a posture of my heart that brings more freedom to my body, mind, spirit, and soul. When I let go, I walk a little taller and feel a little lighter. I stop and breathe. I do less phone calls. More moments in silence and solitude. Less striving, more resting.

When I let go of whatever is restraining me from growing, there is a simultaneous release that takes place. It's a kind of release that causes my hair to run a little wild (and sometimes downright ratchet). I find joy in the present, and I may even break out in a jolly spontaneous dance in my kitchen. My movements become more subtle and passive - less rigid than before. Letting go brings more depth and joy to conversations. Letting go forces me to indulge in the present and releases me to move forward with more clarity and confidence than I had the day before.

When I let go, I stop running around aimlessly, and I'm finally taking a seat to watch God work on my behalf. This creates a greater trust than before, and I see all over again why I was made to be intimate with the lover of my soul. It's for my good.

Growing up, I subconsciously suppressed most of my memories. I wanted to be strong and bring peace to the rest of my family. I think many of us have had this tendency. We carry other people's baggage and deny our own pain in an effort to protect the people closest to us from ever feeling the weight of their own actions. Denying my deepest pain had prevented me from legitimate healing. So, I finally saw the pain for what it was, and I stopped carrying other people's baggage and shame because it was never mine in the first place.

As I'm sure you've learned in your own life, the people closest to us have the most potential to hurt us. Sometimes the best way to love them and ourselves is by giving those relationships to God, dropping all expectations, trusting that in His timing, He will bring healing, and know that you're not responsible for anyone except for yourself. At the end of the day, we all stand before God and give an account for our own lives.

It's freeing to let go of expectations on people. We're all human, we all make mistakes, and we all need grace.

Aging with Grace

Forgiveness and knowing the health of your own heart are not things you typically hear people talking about these days. On the contrary, we're hearing an excessiveness of lies, divisiveness, and corruption happening. There's never been an easier time to get offended about something, hold a grudge, and shut people out.

The world often tells us that grudges and revenge are the answer. The voice of the enemy tells us that we deserve to be bitter, and it can be so tempting at times. But holding grudges doesn't do us any good.

Guilt and shame don't do us any good either. When I'm walking in guilt and shame, I'm depriving myself of the healing and forgiveness available through the cross. Guilt and shame isolate us and bring condemnation. Guilt and shame keep us from seeing ourselves for who God has made us to be.

Shame covers your face from revealing the radiance and beauty that is in you. I promise you, it's in you. We all have beauty in us that is not in us to embarrass us; rather, it is there to shine, which indeed brings glory to God.

True beauty becomes more unexplainable the more you take a glance because it's a beauty that points back to the one who created it. It is a beauty that shouldn't be locked in a cage because it's untamable. It is the kind of beauty that springs up from your soul that you didn't know existed until you honestly face whatever is causing you anxiety, legitimately forgive whoever has wronged you, and let go.

When I observe elderly people, I see the contrast between people who are bitter and those who aren't more clearly than I see in young people. I think it's because they have had so many decisions in their lives leading up to that moment and more and more opportunities to either soften or harden. If they're bitter, it has sucked the life out of them.

The ones who aren't bitter are the ones who have undeniably let go. The steps that they take are light. Their words are kind. I know there are many in between on this spectrum, but I have come to appreciate the people who truly have let go. The ones who know without a shadow of a doubt that God is enough. You know, the old people who aren't control freaks. The ones who will hop in an uber with you without having any idea what the destination will be. (Yes, Gudrun did that with me on many occasions).

Reliance Drive

In the beginning of that year, I lost my job. Then, I lost

my car. My groceries among other things even got stolen. I thought, "when will I catch a break?" It seems to be in those times that God surprises me most. The times where I don't know where my next meal is coming from or how I'll pay the bills... and then miraculously like He always does, God comes like the rain and showers me with His provision.

First, He gave me a stable car. During the month that I didn't have a car, my kind friends Kaylin and Mark let me drive their Prius. Then, one of my best friend's parents randomly shared my story with a couple from their church who, after hearing my story, felt like they should sell their very nice Toyota Highlander to me for thousands of dollars under its value. My friend's parents then decided to buy it for me and told me I could make small payments to them when I was able. Then soon after that, they gave me the car for free.

Then I got three jobs. You might be thinking, "you were chronically ill - how on earth did you work three jobs?" After receiving consistent treatment for almost the entire year before, my health was in a much more stable place than it had been in a long time. God strengthened me supernaturally and showed me how much strength I had in Him.

Then I was given a solid place to call home. If you have chronic illness, you know how detrimentally important your environment is to your health. In the apartment I was sharing with some friends, I began to notice that whenever I would be home, my brain would start functioning extremely slow, I'd be depressed, and pain levels would increase. Every morning became a more intense struggle to get out of bed and just walk out the door. Then I found a bunch of hidden black mold in the bathroom.

Desperate for a change, I toured an apartment located on a street with a name I won't forget: Reliance Drive. As I walked up three flights of stairs and then another flight to get to the bedroom, there it was. A peaceful refuge high above the trees and the noise, with the bright sun beaming through its towering windows, was the room where I was about to be spending lots of time healing in for the next year and a half. I was drenched with peace as I sensed God say, "see Lauren, I have something better for you. Trust me."

That's what He always does in due time. He pulls us out of something that we think is good for us and carries us into something even better that's filled with more purpose. Has there ever been a time in your own life where God gave you something better than you imagined for yourself?

Jesus cares about the details. He has always been standing there watching what's been happening in our lives. He knows our hurts and longings. He hasn't forgotten.

Reliance is quite a word. It means trust, confidence, faith, belief, conviction. After moving into my own apartment, I became convicted of where my reliance truly was. *"I thought I already was fully dependent on you, Lord."* But as He showed me my heart – all its intricate insecurities, wounds, and details – I saw that there were still areas that I didn't want to depend on Jesus in. I preferred to rely on myself, but I heard, *"I assure you that if you want to continue walking with me, this must change."* He was asking me to rely on Him more.

It was there in the quietness of my soul that I began the painful process of letting some of the people I held dearest to my heart go. I let go of expectations on myself to maintain unhealthy relationships anymore. I learned that sometimes, people aren't well; that sometimes they truly don't want to be well, and that I must guard my heart in order to stay well.

A Greater Healing

I expected to be entirely healed by the end of that year. I could not understand why I was still waking up feeling weak and sore and miserable. "God, I thought you promised this to me. Where are you?"

Sometimes, we put expectations and timelines on circumstances that we're not meant to because the circumstances are out of our control. Setting goals and making plans can all be great things in the proper context, but chronic illness throws a wrench in the gears during some of the most inconvenient times - then again, when is it ever convenient to be bedridden? We're left feeling empty and disappointed in God.

Maybe a greater healing had taken place that past year that was going to impact the trajectory of my life drastically more than a physical healing ever could have. Maybe that healing had been in my soul. Though it didn't make sense at the time, maybe the suffering *was* for my good. Maybe the suffering in my body was allowing me to slow down and grieve all the pain from my childhood that I had carried into adulthood. Maybe lyme disease was the exact thing God was using to heal my heart.

Like a string on a yo-yo, letting go allows your soul to unravel from all the ways you unknowingly allowed it to get all knotted up over the years in the depths of your fragile heart. As I begin to let Jesus meticulously undo the knots and let the string loose, I see a sparkling beauty inside of my soul. My soul, which, after further inspection, is of *deep* value to God.

The more I let go, the more I know that He's all around me. He's right here with you too, my friend, sitting with you in humility, desiring to guide your steps, desiring to meet you wherever you are.

Grieving Childhood Trauma

It's autumn again. The trees are going bare, and sidewalks are dressed in countless tints of warm-colored leaves. I grab my sweater and walk toward a grave that's labeled "my childhood." I take a seat in front of it.

Memories flood my mind from the home in Tennessee that my parents and us three kids lived in for a short time right before my parent's divorce. That home the last place I was around my dad much.

I remember the doorways of each room and the large

turtle that my sister and I met one day in the backyard and painted his shell. I remember locking myself in the bathroom and my dad threatening me if I decided to call the cops on him.

I remember my dad breaking down the bedroom door and knocking over our Legos as mom and us three kids huddled in bed together. I remember many days playing with those same Legos on the bedroom floor of my sister's room while eating frozen raspberries and cookies, the only two foods in the house after my mom left my dad. I was terrified, not knowing whether or not my dad was coming home before my mom picked me up on her way home from work.

Many other memories flood my mind, but I'll spare you the details. I share this part of my story because I think people crave the raw and emotional parts of our stories more than we think. We, as humans, can handle the truth. In fact, I think we prefer it. I didn't want to put this part in my book, and yet, now, I see that this part of my story is not the part I'm supposed to hide.

I recently heard from a doctor that most of our emotions are formed in the womb. This occurs during the last three months of pregnancy. If a mom becomes upset during her pregnancy, the baby feels that. If her husband is abusive, the baby feels that. Trauma can start in the womb and have enormous ripple effects.

Physical trauma doesn't even have to happen to the mom for it to occur in the fetus. If the mom is under a great deal of stress, experiencing chronic guilt, or toxic emotional trauma – that can compute into the very fiber of the fetus' genetic makeup.

Sometimes we wonder why we aren't healing. And yet we keep shoving the memories that shaped us at a deep level. Or, like me, we barely remember anything.

I'm not shoving the memories that I do remember anymore. I'm processing them with my counselor. And I'm praying all I know to pray: "God, please take this pain and make something beautiful out of it."

Sometimes when we get to know people, we judge them and make assumptions about them. What we don't know is how trauma has affected them. We probably have no idea that they've even been through trauma. We don't know the grief they're carrying and all its complexities. What if, from now on, we assumed that everyone we know has been through some sort of trauma? I think we'd have a lot more compassion.

As I sit at the gravestone of my childhood, tears drizzle down my cheeks. The gravestone demands proper grieving. It demands letting the memories flood my mind and then flush out of me like a bag of toxins.

I've been holding back from proper grieving for 16 years. I haven't wanted to feel all the anger that's associated with this grief. I've been scared of it. But now, alone in my house, all the anger is coming out of me like a cup of hot water pouring out into a garden until all the water has been soaked up by the dirt in order for something new and life-giving to grow from that dirt. "Were you there?" I ask Jesus. He says, "yes." I say, "why didn't you do anything about it?" All I hear is, "I love you."

Grieving is certainly a part of healing. When grief doesn't take place, we typically hurt the people around us in the process. We hurt ourselves. We take our anger out on everything but the actual source of anger.

So, the next time I have rage and anger, I'm coming back to this graveyard. I'll sit here as long as it takes for the grief to come up and out so that God can refill those spaces of anger and hurt with His love.

The Father's Delight

It was Easter morning. For the years leading up to this day, I had spent Easter mornings believing that God would heal me that day. Don't ask me why; that's just what I believed.

This year was different than the years prior. I wasn't

joyful. I was worn out from physical pain.

I dragged my body to the bathroom, turned on the water, sat on the floor of my shower, and cried. And then I felt Jesus say, "look up." As I looked up, I could feel and sense beautiful Jesus sitting there in the shower right front of me, intently looking into my eyes. I felt Him say, "I am so proud of you; your heart is so beautiful." I then felt the Father come in front of me and sit to the right of Jesus. I felt them say, "we incline our ears to you. We love to hear your voice. We intently listen to you."

Then, I felt two angels come behind me, one on each shoulder. My shoulders automatically drew back, and I was breathing deeper. Then I felt the Holy Spirit come to the left side of the back of my head - somewhere where I typically experience pain. They all looked at me intently. Then they came closer, and all five of them gave me a massive hug. Again, God reiterated, "Lauren, we incline our ears to you. Speak up. We love to hear your voice. We are here. We are proud of you." I said, "please don't leave." They said, "We aren't going anywhere."

Encountering the King of Kings is the only way that I'm able to conclude that it's better to feel the effects of a debilitating disease and be close to Jesus than be healed and not have Him. Jesus brings transformation through tragedy. He uses the most devastating occurrences for my good. Jesus is who makes life rich and meaningful and the way it was meant to be lived. I hear Him say, "I am the LORD, that is my name. I will finish the work of healing in your body. I will take care of you."

To hear the words, "I'm so proud of you" from my Father keeps me grounded. Those words keep me going. There's nothing like living in the Father's delight.

God is with you and me. He's omnipresent. He can sit with me while simultaneously sitting with you. He's better, grander, and more out of the box than we think He is. Today, if we hear Him, let us not harden our hearts. Jesus looks at you and me with piercing eyes of love and fire and laughter, and I hear Him say, "just stay here with me. Become like a child here with me again."

You know those times you look back on and have no clue how you managed to get through them? The times that you can barely make your way out or even see anything that lies ahead, and somehow God pulls you out? He surely did that for me.

He picked me up out of the weeds I sat in, and with mud all over my clothes and face, He led me out. He saw what was underneath all the mud. As I frantically paced through that desolate field in the middle of the night, somehow, through the thick grass I couldn't see through anymore, there was a clearing. Jesus took my hand and led me to a meadow.

In my meadow, by God's grace, I see things differently and clearer than I did before. I'm changing, growing, and still letting go. So, I wake up to another day of taking responsibility for what I am responsible for and throwing off my shoulders what wasn't ever meant for me to carry in the first place. How liberating it is to let go. How much more space I have in my heart and how much less I am carrying on my shoulders now.

CHAPTER NINE

Joy Unraveled

"No lion will be there,
Nor any ravenous beast;
They will not be found there.
But only the redeemed will walk there,
And those the Lord has rescued will return.
They will enter Zion with singing;
Everlasting joy will crown their heads.
Gladness and joy will overtake them,
And sorrow and sighing will flee away."
Isaiah 35:9-10 (NIV)

It's funny how God unexpectedly does the things that you completely lost hope for and brings the people you didn't know you needed when you least expect it. Behind the scenes and backdrops, He's moving mountains we don't even see, giving us the desires of our hearts that we forgot we even had.

When I was 25, God surprised me. Big time. Somewhere along my journey, I started to settle into the idea of being single for the rest of my life and maybe adopting children on my own later down the road. Obviously, I still dreamt of prince charming from time to time, but I thought mine probably just wasn't out there. I thought if I ever did find a man who stuck around, I'd never let him fully into my situation.

About seven months after I had moved to Reliance drive and right after a hard break-up, I felt the Lord tell me that I was ready to be a wife. I thought, "well great, but I don't know anybody in the world who's ready to be my husband." And with a laugh, I went on with my day.

Then, I met Andy Murphree. We met at a bonfire at our church in Tennessee. He was wearing a blue and white flannel and had a beard that was much less wild than it is now. We began chatting, and we eventually sat next to each other in front of the fire. Andy was intentional and gentle at the same time, and I had absolute peace sitting next to him on that little log in front of that fire.

There was a commonality and tenderness between us that flourished as time went on. We could talk about our relationships with Jesus for hours at a time, and it was refreshing, to say the least. Being friends with a guy who understood what having a genuine and intimate relationship with Jesus actually meant made me realize how phony most other guys were.

When we were dating, I recall when I first felt something unfamiliar, especially with a male. I felt *safe*. As much as I felt that it wasn't the right time for a serious relationship, God was giving me a peace that I hadn't ever experienced in a romantic relationship.

Our lives seemed to sort of effortlessly fall apart and together all at the same time. Our faces were brighter, and we had aspirations in the most unexpected places of our hearts. We were undoubtedly in love, and God was beginning to use Andy to bring redemption to my story.

It continually became evident that God was leading us towards a life together. There we were, a couple of naive twenty-something-year-olds, taking a hard look at our own brokenness, potential future hardships, lack of finances, weaknesses, imbalances, medical diagnoses... everything.

And whatever it was going to look like - we wanted to face it together.

Humble Beginnings

Andy and I got married on a bright and warm day in October. While my bridesmaids and I were getting ready that morning, what I wanted to do was lay curled up in my bed like I had been wanting to do every day for the last month because of how poor my health was and how little sleep I had been getting. But I didn't talk about it. I didn't know how to talk about it because of how invisible it was to everyone around me.

So, I shut myself alone in a room, and when I came back out, I did my best to brush off the pain I was in. What kept me going that day was knowing that I was marrying the love of my life.

As our pastor Shane told Andy to receive his bride, and the doors flung open for me to step forward with my stepdad by my side, the pain in my body seemed to flood over all my desires to show Andy how excited I was in that moment to be walking down the aisle and marrying him. I felt bare, completely empty, with what felt like very little to offer my husband. I was coming forward as the imperfect and flawed human I am, having a hard time believing someone was committing themselves to be my husband.

If you have chronic illness, I think big moments like your wedding day can be painful reminders of how secretly abnormal your life is. It's as if there's this film constantly over every part of you and suddenly, the moments that you want to be so present and full of life become a fog. But that fog didn't stop me from seeing what mattered. As a light beamed on my groom's face at the end of the aisle, all I could do was gaze into his blue eyes.

As Andy and I danced our way out of our ceremony into the great unknown, although things didn't seem all that different, I knew that something subtle yet miraculous had happened. Though I still had pain in my body, I experienced a new kind of healing and freedom. Marrying a very loving man who cultivated a completely different kind of culture than what I grew up in was the most tangible way of seeing God's promises and redemption in my life.

That evening, I ate an entire gluten-free pizza, drank wine, and danced the night away because I didn't want to let lyme dictate the day. Thankfully, it didn't.

I think that crowns of joy, blessing, and authority fell on our heads that day we become one flesh. Stepping into a Godly marriage that is unified is a strong threat against the enemy. Staying unified together through your trials only makes you stronger.

After trying so hard to control my symptoms and push myself beyond what my body was capable of for months leading up to our wedding day working at a restaurant in order to pay bills, I felt like I had just collapsed from a marathon, and I crashed - *hard*. I struggled to walk to the bathroom most days. We weren't necessarily experiencing "honeymoon bliss."

Pushing myself obviously hadn't done me any good, and it wasn't good for Andy in the long run either. It was no longer only me having to deal with the repercussions of pushing myself beyond my limit anymore, but now my husband was too.

That day was the beginning of learning some unexpected lessons that come with being a spouse while battling chronic illness. These lessons are unique and deeply humbling because most things I thought would be good for my husband before we got married aren't good for him. Andy has felt the same way on countless occasions. We want to love each other so well, yet loving one another with God's heart and eyes can look extremely different from what we think love looks like at times.

Here's one of the lessons I learned: one day, I got so frustrated with my phone because it was barely working anymore. So then, I hit it against the dashboard of my car as if that was going to help it work. And I thought to myself,

"Lauren, this is how you treat your body sometimes. You expect so much out of it, and you get angry with it when it doesn't comply with your expectations. You're at odds with yourself. Start showing yourself greater kindness and self-compassion. That's your weapon."

Learning Love

My lack of grace towards my body, all my expectations I put on it, and all the expectations I put on what marriage was going to look like made our marriage a lot harder. I was stuck in a performance-based mentality. If I achieved more, I felt better about myself.

I won't forget the words of our marriage counselor during that season. He said, "Lauren, you don't have to be super sex wife." Not sure where I picked that mentality up, but I think after hearing so many Christian women talk about it, what I felt was *pressure*. That sex was supposed to happen all the time, and if it didn't, there was something wrong with us.

Ever since a young age, I always wanted to prove that "I can do it," whatever the challenge would be. In my friendships and relationships, I'd usually strive to be the best friend anyone ever had, the best girlfriend, and now I was striving to be the best wife. The truth of the matter is that I can't do anything on my own and can only be the wife my husband truly needs when I'm truly relying on Jesus. The truth is that I am solely valued because God says that I am.

I sensed God say to me in that season, "I don't value you for what you do. I've placed you here. I'm not concerned about your paycheck; I'm concerned about your heart. Trust that I will do miraculous and beautiful things through your pain. You haven't missed the mark."

He's after my heart. Not my appearance, how much money I make, what kind of car I drive, or what kind of clothes I wear. He wants me in all my imperfections, just as I am – no strings attached.

My expectations being met by what actually mattered

was a tiny representation of what marriage legitimately looks like: holy and sanctifying. And until I stepped into a covenant with my husband, I didn't understand what marriage meant. You don't get a dress rehearsal in marriage; you just keep showing up. You keep asking God for wisdom, guidance, and strength. You keep asking God for His heart for your spouse.

Marriage can be exciting, challenging, comical, humbling, painful, healing, growing, fun, and messy all at the same time. You keep being seen up close and personal in all your ugly moments, and you can't hide your pain no matter how hard you try. You become unraveled before another human being as they become unraveled at the same time and all you can do is sit there on the floor together in your brokenness, holding different parts of your heart, knowing that who you're in front of is holding different parts of their hearts too; knowing that you need Jesus even more than you did before.

It took me a good while to believe in my heart that Andy was not going anywhere. I'm not used to people in it for the long haul. Having both come from divorced families and childhood trauma, only God could bring two hurting people together and create something beautiful. Without a shadow of a doubt, our marriage is a miracle.

Andy is a remarkable, strong, and humble man. No human has more of my honor and respect. He's changed my life in the best of ways. He stands in the gap for me. He lays down his life for me. He treats me in a way I've never been treated by anyone. He cherishes me, honors me, and shows me deep love. He is God's greatest gift to me.

I could write a whole lot about how building a life together has looked different than we thought it would, like how Andy threw his back out the night of our wedding carrying me up our apartment stairs, how we felt like old people on our honeymoon and slept for 14 hours most nights, how we missed our flight coming home from our honeymoon at the crack of dawn, our crazy adventures during our layover in Tampa like sitting on our suitcase in the ghetto, broke, to being served the same champagne that was picked out to be in the White House that same night. That was all within our first week of marriage, so you can imagine how many priceless stories we have. God has worked through everything in hilarious and magnificent ways.

When we said, "I do," we obviously had no idea how my health would be in the future. We didn't know that it would decline or that Andy's health would decline too. We had no idea what we were diving into, but God met us in our weakest moments and taught us how to love - what we're still learning how to do today.

Love is most certainly a choice. It doesn't always come naturally by any means. As we continue to grow as individuals together, as we grow healthier, and as we continue in our journey as husband and wife - we're seeing new life emerging from the dirt. Though we may not feel it at times, the seeds we once planted are beginning to show their tiny sprouts.

Seeds

Autumn is a special time to me. Many Autumns have tended to be seasons of hope and beauty in my life. That's when I met my husband; that's when I married him. That's when we settled into our first house of our own together out here on a country road in Colorado.

People tend to be in a better mood in the Fall. The hot summer sun has ceased, and it isn't too cold yet to where people are feeling achy and annoyed at how freezing it is outside. As we watch crisp leaves gracefully sweep across the windshields of our cars, as we cuddle up next to crackling fires that make our clothes and hair smell like smoke, and scents of apple pie seep through the vents of our homes - hope is entering our hearts again.

We pull out the flannels and burnt orange sweaters that have been stuffed away in our closets; scarves wrap around our necks as warm hugs, and we are ushered into a fresh stillness as we hold a hot cup of something delightful. We sit around the table, come up with new facial expressions for our pumpkins, and we giggle. No matter how busy life can get, we do our best to have this childlike faith and wonder in the midst of all the tragedy that we see happening in our world. We do our best to make time for the ones we love because they are God's gifts to us.

Even though Autumn is one of the plants withering away and the green trees going bare - it is also a season of full maturity, of harvest, of beauty, and thanks. I am breathing in this Fall like it's my first Fall. I'm breathing in expectation for good things because, just like Paul says, suffering results in hope. I'm seeing His faithfulness after a long season of pain and grief. The tears I shed are different; they are filled with awe and gratitude and life.

There's much to learn from a seed - a tiny yet powerful unit of reproduction. What makes seed-growing successful? For starters, they need light. These small seedlings need more light than full-grown plants. I imagine all the small seeds in our souls that are preparing to spring forth a garden of fruit, a garden that exudes the character of Christ. Those little seeds need extra light. They need to bask in the goodness of vitamin D and be watered by what brings life.

I believe that there are seeds in all of us that either bloom or die. The good seeds aren't meant to stay seeds. How do we allow them to grow? They need consistent care. We can't just leave them unattended, or they will not grow or flourish or be shown to the world. They must be nourished.

Seeds start small, as do many things in life. Think about a man and a woman in love, the businessman or the lawyer who was told that they couldn't get anywhere in life, or thousands of other stories and scenarios. They all started somewhere. With a seed. Those people who fell in love started with a moment, and then there were thousands of moments after that where they chose to love each other even when the going got hard. Their seed of love bloomed into a flower and then into a garden. The business owner persisted even when what they were doing did not make any logical sense to others. The lawyer went to law school driving a beater car in a city that she strongly disliked, but she persisted in her hard work because she believed she could, and so she did. She bloomed where she had been planted, regardless of how much she disliked the soil.

I know that seeds are associated with Spring but bear with me. From Autumn until Spring, nobody can see what's happening beneath the surface or how the seeds survive. Nobody sees how the seeds change in order for them to be prepared for what they will come to produce in the Spring.

Some experts say that wildflower seeds are best planted in the Fall. This is for multiple reasons: the gardeners can take their time during the Fall, the weed seeds that are usually ramping around the wildflowers in the Spring have gone dormant, and these wildflowers bloom earlier than the ones you would plant in the Spring.

I like to think of my walk with God in this season as me being a wildflower and Him being the gardener. He's taking his time on me; He's allowing the weeds of lyme disease that have entangled themselves around me to finally go dormant and wither away; He's caused me to grow in places that were not natural to me. He's making me untamed yet gentle; He's making me free.

You have seeds inside of you. Ideas, dreams, talents - things that make you come alive. You've learned how to tame them, maybe even crush them - how to make yourself more acceptable to the world. But what I encourage in you today is to turn your gaze to the good seeds again. Lay the seeds before Jesus. Ask Him to nourish them and flourish them.

Remember that the worms - representing the trials of life - whatever they may be, they enrich the soil; the garden is not the same without the worms. Don't do what I have done so many times and see the worms as dirty or meaningless, aerating the soil of your life. Remember tribulation's treasures. Remember that the kingdom of God is upside down.

Blessed are the poor in spirit, for theirs is the kingdom of Heaven.
Blessed are those who mourn, for they will be comforted.
Blessed are the meek, for they will inherit the earth. Blessed are those who hunger and thirst for righteousness, for they will be filled.
Blessed are the merciful, for they will be shown mercy.
Blessed are the pure in heart, for they will see God.
Blessed are the peacemakers, for they will be called children of God.
Blessed are those who are persecuted because of righteousness, for theirs is the kingdom of Heaven
Matthew 5: 1-10 (NIV)

When the world thinks we are a lost cause, God calls us blessed.

Persist in what He's called you to, friend. Look for the light - it will illuminate your darkness. Walk the narrow way. Be bold.

All this talk of hope and light and Jesus may be too much for your wounded heart and tired eyes today, but I assure you that what you long for from Him is possible. "The light shines in the darkness, and the darkness has not overcome it." (John 1:5 NIV)

It's Gonna Rain Joy

One afternoon while Andy and I were still fresh newlyweds, as I was trying to get some things done in our living room, pain and fatigue plagued me. I sat on the couch with a sigh. My overachiever mentality had gotten the best of me again, and I needed to call it quits. Then one of my favorite artists, Melissa Helser, came to mind. I got on

Spotify and discovered her latest song at the time, called "White as Snow."

In the song, she repeats the phrase, "it's gonna rain joy." This is the phrase that she would sing to herself year after year as she struggled with (and still struggles with, I believe) a skin/bone disease, chronic pain... an imprisonment in her own body that she was first diagnosed with at the age of eighteen years old. Now, years down the road, with two teenagers, an incredible ministry with her husband, Jonathan, she releases "White As Snow." A powerful yet soft-spoken song that you can't help but feel how she looks to the Lord in her pain every day and how she fights in the spiritual realm against what attacks her body. In the middle of the song, she says,

> I breathe in deep what You've promised
> And let all the pain fall off my shoulders
> It's gonna rain joy

Those few words hit my soul and gave me hope again. We don't realize how powerful our words, our simple melodies, or our lives can be for God's glory. We can't always see the ripple effects of our own breakthroughs.

I was on the phone the other day with one of my family members, Jackie. When I was a kid, Jackie and her husband, Doug, allowed my mom and us three kids to live with them and their big family while my parents were separated. I don't remember for how long, but I know it was for a good while and a sacrifice for their family. Their generosity to our family now almost 20 years ago still speaks to me today.

In a recent conversation with Jackie, she said, "people see you, Lauren. Although you may not hear from them, they do." She went on to tell me that the day I posted something on my instagram about Melissa's song nearly two years prior, Jackie looked up the song. That is the very song that has helped get her through some of her darkest days over the last year and half.

Thank you, Melissa, for making your music. You have no idea how much your music has impacted my own life and countless others.

As I continued to listen to Melissa's song, I grabbed my paints and a blank canvas and painted what I had just envisioned while listening to the song: a baby blue canvas with paint splattered all over it and the words "it's gonna rain joy" spread across it. As I continued to paint that baby blue canvas, I felt the Lord say to me, "I am bringing you redemption now. Let the rain wash over you. Believe it, my child. Live in it, my child. Delight, my child. Drink deeply and be satisfied. Let yourself be free to dance, sing, paint... you are free." I am free. My body and brain are still learning it, but that is the truth,

That canvas is currently hanging up in our home in Colorado, a reminder every day of God's promise of joy over us, among other promises, like the children we will have one day.

Jesus was there in that 700 square foot apartment that we lived in our first nine months of marriage in Franklin, Tennessee. Sometimes sitting in a chair in our home peacefully, sometimes filled with laughter. He was always engaged with us whenever we chose to engage with Him. Never worried. Always present.

Joy is not necessarily what we think when we initially think of the word. True joy of the Lord has nothing to do with circumstances or feelings. It is not always a smile on your face. It's deep, it's raw; it can even be sorrowful at times, yet still rejoicing.

That rejoicing may not look like singing at the top of your lungs and praising God. It may come in the form of loving your spouse. It may come in the form of getting out of bed to another day of chronic pain and parts of your body feeling like they barely work anymore and still having gratitude in your heart though it doesn't come naturally.

It's gonna rain joy, my friend. I have friends with such unspeakable pain - miscarriages, losses of loved ones, depression, anxiety, effects of suicide, cancer, you name it. We see repercussions of sin here on earth everywhere we turn.

All flesh is like grass - it withers away in a blink of an eye. Our lives are like vapors. *And yet,* God cares intimately and deeply for every single one of us.

"For my thoughts are not your thoughts, neither are your ways my ways, declares the Lord. For as the heavens are higher than the earth, so are my ways higher than your ways and my thoughts than your thoughts.

For as the rain and the snow come down from heaven and do not return there but water the earth, making it bring forth and sprout, giving seed to the sower and bread to the eater, so shall my word be that goes out from my mouth; it shall not return to me empty, but it shall accomplish that which I purpose, and shall succeed in the thing for which I sent it.

"For you shall go out in joy and be led forth in peace; the mountains and the hills before you shall break forth into singing, and all the trees of the field shall clap their hands. Instead of the thorn shall come up the cypress; instead of the brier shall come up the myrtle; and it shall make a name for the Lord, an everlasting sign that shall not be cut off."

Isaiah 55:8-13 (ESV)

CHAPTER TEN

Newlyweds in Quarantine

"Come, let us return to the Lord,
He has torn us to pieces
But He will heal us; He has injured us
But He will bind up our wounds.
After two days He will revive us;
On the third day He will restore us,
That we may live in His presence.
Let us acknowledge the Lord Let us press on to
acknowledge Him.
As surely as the sun rises, He will appear; He will come to
us like the winter rains,
Like the spring rains that water the earth."
Hosea 6: 1-3 (NIV)

As we can all attest to, 2020 was a crazy year. About six months into marriage, just as we were getting used to the adjustment of living together, the world around us got shaken up. At the very beginning of March, a deadly tornado ripped through Nashville. Countless homes were destroyed, and many lost their lives. The Nashville community pulled up their bootstraps, came together, and served their neighbors.

Then came the word that we all could use some counseling for these days: covid. And then came another strain. And then came more deaths reported on a daily basis. And then came fear.

On a personal level, then came fights between Andy and I. Then came hurtful words that penetrated our fresh love. Then came dishonesty about how we felt. Then came exhaustion.

Then came assumptions, disunity, and now comes the good part... ultimately a realization of a lack of freedom in our own hearts. Freedom from fear, freedom from insecurities, freedom from lies in our heads. Those things in ourselves we didn't know how to heal from crept up, and the enemy was using them to bring disharmony in our marriage.

I thought, "no, not us. This shouldn't be happening." My young married self said, "we've already worked through so much emotional baggage for our age," not understanding how much more growth needed to happen inside of us in order to have a healthy marriage.

We were going through a hurdle in our relationship, and it was for our good. We sought counsel from our church leaders. We cried, we sat in our brokenness, and God met us. He was using covid and the fears and unknowns that came with it in order to sanctify and ultimately change us.

Maybe God used that time to change you and your marriage, too. In a moment, everyone seemed to be facing a desert of some sort, whether it was in their employment, health, or marriage, to name a few. Maybe depression came out of nowhere for you. Maybe you experienced unbearable loneliness. Maybe you're still experiencing it.

Every single person, not only nationally but globally, was facing uncertainty about what their future looked like. We could no longer go and do all the fast-paced activities that were always deemed as normal pre-covid. It was as if God was telling the entire world to slow down and get back to the basics.

I was highly concerned about how covid affected me more than anything or anyone else because I was afraid. I wanted to be protected and safe.

I thought, "What in the world, God? I just got this job that is a perfect fit for me; we found a medical treatment that we are finally seeing good results from that I can't go to anymore, and the career I started pursuing is now impossible to pursue. How can everything be put on hold, and how can you allow me to go through this, right when it was all turning around?" He patiently listened.

What I was forgetting was that every single person was facing the coronavirus. Sure, they may have not had my medical history, but some of them had a lot harder circumstances than I did.

I think every Christian in the world was experiencing new levels of spiritual warfare when covid happened; I just don't think many of us knew it at the time. When covid came and changed our world, satan was turning up the amp with his attacks on God's people. Fear was trying to sneakily maneuver its way into our homes, and for many families, it succeeded.

The Bigger Picture

That March, as the news rampantly bombarded our homes with panic, fear and confusion became a national norm. The building that Andy worked in had their first confirmed case of covid. Then a day after the confirmed case, Andy came home feeling feverish and shortness of breath - the things the news was saying weren't good signs. Before I knew it, I was experiencing those same symptoms.

When fear and death tried to skulk their way into our home, we made a conscious decision that fear has no place in our lives. Sure, with autoimmune diagnoses or the frailty of life that every one of us face, we can certainly become fearful of everything in the world - but isn't that exactly what the enemy wants?

When my emotions stopped running the show, I began to see the distinctly bigger picture that was going on. God was using what was going on in the world to not only improve our marriage but also give us new and more sustainable rhythms.

Andy and I lived in the Stone Age in our first apartment. We didn't have wi-fi for the first six months. We had a small TV that Andy's dad gave him years ago with one of those goofy antennas and the most basic cable that we played GameCube on together for fun.

It's good to get back to the basics. In a time where we can access any video we desire at any moment, scroll through social media all hours of the day and night, and fill our brains with whatever we please every day, what if we went against the norm? What if we regularly fasted from social media? What if we chose to turn our phones off before getting in bed? What if we decided to look in other people's eyes more than we do on Instagram? What if we intentionally chose to be present every day?

Take a moment to sink and settle into wherever you are right now. Try to release any tension you're feeling in your body and mind. Forget about tasks and getting back emails that aren't currently an urgent matter. Be present with yourself.

Now, take a deep breath from your belly. And another, and another. Now, where were we?

Simplicity and limitations give more room to be in solitude with God, be present with those around us, and tend to what we've been given right in front of us - instead of the outlets that are wasting our precious time and energy.

A few weeks into quarantine, I stepped into what was a good and needed season for my heart. It was a time of mere acceptance: acceptance of the pain I've experienced in my body every day, acceptance of who I am instead of believing lies, and acceptance of the life that was right in front of me. I could embrace that life more. I could stop guilt-tripping myself over my limitations. I could choose to be empowered. I could choose to empower others.

Before the world shut down, I wasn't aware of the refining that my heart was still in need of. I forgot that refinement is a process that doesn't stop when we think it should. God's timeline is different than mine.

I didn't realize how much pressure I was putting on myself, how hard I was putting up defenses and trying to hide my lyme symptoms from basically everyone. Many times, the pressure I put on myself prevented me from loving people as well as being "seen" and loved because I didn't let people fully know me. I thought if I showed lyme in the way that I walked or if I tried to make my brain work faster in conversations with friends, that I was being strong, but I was in denial.

Quarantine helped me see a much bigger picture that I was too blind to see before in all my striving. I realized that there was a different way of life I was called to that was filled with more simplicity.

Most things that I had grown concerned about didn't, in fact, matter. I was desperately reaching around, trying to pile more responsibilities on my shoulders that would've shown to the world, "I got this." Those concerns and responsibilities didn't have eternal value though, and only made me feel more conflicted inside.

One day while Andy was outside on his lunch break, he saw a bunny in the corner of his eye. He then felt the Lord say to him, "be like the bunny." As Andy dissected what the life of a bunny looks like, it was nothing magnificent. They eat carrots, sleep, hop around, have sex, then eat and sleep some more. They don't add any real value to the world, but God still sees them as a gift.

Bunnies look like frightened little creatures, just hopping from one safe piece of grass to the next. But God cares for them despite what they lack. He doesn't care about their productivity. He's just waiting to lavish His love on them in all the unexpected moments, to remind them that He loves them and there's nothing they can do about it.

He loves you, and there's nothing you can do about it.

The Value of Friendships

I've always valued friendships, especially when you're truly able to be vulnerable with each other. You never have to stick around and stay friends with people, yet when you choose to keep sticking around and being friends through the highs and lows of life, something happens. You care about each other. You get to speak into one another's lives because you know each other on a deep level. God can use friends in unique ways to pull us out of the holes we are buried in. They help us see things more clearly.

During quarantine, we all had the option to completely check out of life other than for the zoom calls or occasional "social" things we go to do only if we suited up in our masks that covered our smiles and half of our faces. It seemed easier to drop friendships, no longer stay connected, and not feel the consequences of any of it because we didn't have to see anybody anymore.

So many relationships have fallen apart these last couple of years. When everyone went into quarantine, it was as if all the crap underneath the surface of many people's planners and facades came out and completely hit the fan. The divorce rate ramped up, and face-to-face interactions with people plummeted to an all-time low. More walking on eggshells. More division. More people isolated and afraid.

Maybe some of us did check out of life or drop friendships. Sometimes it's just easier that way, right? Or is it? Friendships aren't a necessity to life, so no need to invest in them, right? Is community something that drains us, or does it enrich our lives? Is being vulnerable with friends we trust a terrible idea, or can it be a healthy, positive thing?

There's typically a softening that takes place in vulnerability with safe people. Compassion rises as we learn one another's stories more. I know that when I'm on the phone with one of my friends, our voices tend to soften a little more toward one another when we are being vulnerable. It's something that isn't required of either of us, yet we choose to get real because we trust and value one another. As our facades fall off our shoulders, freedom begins to brew. It's like vulnerability breeds this whole new world. We can sit with each other and not have to fake anything anymore. Vulnerable friendships help shape us into who we were always meant to be.

I find many times that after being vulnerable with a friend I trust, I begin to have more grace and acceptance towards myself. I begin to see things more clearly as they are and no longer downplay or try to put some pretty bow on my aching heartaches anymore. As I practice acceptance in certain areas of my life, it tends to bleed into other areas. I'm able to drop false narratives that I have held onto in the past, and my interactions and life begin to change. I become less cynical and more kind.

God has given me great strength by being vulnerable with the right friends. Through trial and error, I've learned to be more vulnerable with the people who have earned my trust and to guard my heart with people who haven't. Learning this has helped my emotional and mental health exponentially.

Friends are important. But when I say friends, I don't mean people who we never hang out with. In a time where it's all about platforms and communicating more through social media than in real life, can we just take a moment to think about how weird this is? "How many followers do you have?" I recently heard someone say, "once you've had a relationship with someone via social media for years..." let's just stop right there. If relationship means sending small messages here or there or commenting on a photo of someone you've never met, I don't want a "relationship."

I want connection. True connection doesn't happen by looking at other people's lives through a screen. It happens in the subtle moments of being present with someone and learning who they genuinely are at their core – what you can only learn by being in their presence.

I want to put my baseball cap on and meet a friend at the park. I want to take a stroll in nature together and talk about the real matters of life. I want to look into my friend's eyes and confess my sins like being critical of my husband (which usually starts with me being critical of myself) or isolating myself, or staying angry. I want to sit in the grass and get down to the nitty-gritties of it all. I want to be sharpened by my friends. I don't want superficial. I want real. I think deep down, we all do.

Spirals of Sadness and Grief

At the beginning of 2020, I went to see a new lyme specialist for the first time in a while. He had no website or office with a sign on it. He was under the radar because he didn't want people to know about him, only referrals of people who had already seen him. This is because some practitioners who have legitimately helped people with lyme have had incredibly awful things done to them because of it.

He told me that borrelia had taken an extreme toll on my body. Old co-infections were active again. There were different markers for how bad it can get, and he said he saw lyme patients usually have one marker or maybe two, but that's it. I had nine.

He suggested I use his rife machine as a part of my treatment. I had always been hesitant to use a rife machine for various reasons, but mainly because of the scary stories I heard of what lyme patients had to endure if it wasn't done correctly. I was willing to try anything at that point despite the risks, and more importantly: I had peace from God.

After a few months of treatment and seemingly making some progress, my health collapsed again. Maybe it was stress. Maybe it was the fact that I couldn't use the rife machine for a time because the office was shut down due to covid. Who knows.

When you feel like God is doing something in your life and you still believe it after believing it hundreds of other times, so many years, and then you don't see the results you thought would happen, it's hard not to feel foolish. It's hard to keep believing. To all my friends who are still waiting on their healing, who are still waiting for everything to change, who have been trying to get pregnant but haven't, I am so sorry for your continual grief.

I imagine those who walked around the walls of Jericho felt foolish, too.

It's very challenging to know how to grieve appropriately or at all, for that matter, if you're still in the middle of turmoil and trauma. How can you grieve what's still going on? How is it possible to be "okay" in social settings when you feel like you're barely holding on anymore?

After Easter, I fell into a spiral of sadness. The little glimmers of hope I had experienced in the early Spring days were covered with a downpour of grief. I didn't want to talk to friends anymore. I didn't know how to grieve everything anymore. I was just putting one foot in front of the other.

The rife machine that had once been healing to me was now making me feel worse, and I wasn't recovering from the sessions. I don't remember any breaks from the pain or itchiness under my skin. I would itch my legs at night until they would bleed and scab. My face and different parts of my body felt like they were going numb all the time. I fell asleep and woke up to shooting pains all over my body. Every night began to feel like a nightmare. We were in need of clarity. We were in need of a move of God.

Then I saw another lyme specialist I had heard about with a new treatment method that had been the miracle drug for thousands of other lyme patients, including himself. Out of all things in the world, it was a drug for alcoholics called disulfiram (AKA Antabuse). Just to clarify, I haven't had a drink since Andy and I's anniversary a year ago (regret) because alcohol feeds lyme, nor have I ever had any sort of addiction to alcohol.

After a vigorous amount of researching the drug for over a month, I decided to take a whack at disulfiram. I was desperate for relief. I followed everything my doctor told me to do when I started the drug. I went very low and slow with the dosages, avoided all yeast, anything fermented, all products with alcohol – this included hand sanitizer, the thing that was required to be used nearly everywhere, among other foods and products aside from my already extremely strict diet I'd been on for years. I followed all the rules and thought that disulfiram would be my miracle drug and that I'd finally be able to live a normal life.

It was somewhere just before hitting the 200mg mark that I had the closest thing I've ever had to a mental breakdown. Nobody else saw it, but it scared me. I stopped the drug, but the symptoms and damage, such as peripheral and cranial neuropathy (one of my least favorite symptoms) from the drug persisted.

That season, along with the next, and the next, and the entire following year was inordinately tough for us. Andy's health declined. We both got angry at God from time to time. In our weakest moments, we got frustrated with each other. We've learned that it's much better to express all your anger and confusion to God than to your spouse because only God can handle all of it.

When you try in your best efforts to help someone heal, and they don't, that is devastating. And when you are the one with life-altering health conditions, when you put so much effort and energy and all your resources into getting well, and you don't, that is devastating too.

I still don't understand why. I still know God is working behind the scenes. I still believe that on the third day, Jesus rose again and that He died so that I can live and have everlasting life. That is a promise, and getting to spend eternity with Him will make it all worth it.

God's Grace on My Life

A couple of months later, my mobility became more limited to the point that when we were trying to meet up with someone at the park one day, I nonchalantly mentioned to Andy how helpful a wheelchair would be. Then, that same someone we were going to meet, who has always been generous, decided to buy me one and surprise us with it. When I saw it come through our apartment door, I felt shocked and a plethora of other emotions. As I sat down in the wheelchair, I broke down and cried for a moment that felt confusing and brought up strong feelings. More than anything else, I felt shame.

I've come to realize that the worse that I'm feeling in my body, I tend to carry more shame. My brain remembers that shame. That shame grew when I got hooked on narcotics for a year when I was 20 years old because I knew no other way to deal with the pain. That same shame grew whenever I spent other people's money on treatments that didn't help me. I felt like I was failing those people because I was still sick. More than anything, the shame grew when the people I trusted most did not believe what I was going through.

The reality is that the people who helped me get treatment weren't mad at me that I was still sick; they gave out of love and generosity in their hearts. And the reality is that the shame spiral I had been in was never God's intent or heart for me.

Back to that day when a kind someone gave me a wheelchair. As my frail body sat in that wheelchair, after fighting so hard for so long, it felt a little bit like a defeat and like I was giving up, especially with the fact that I still had legs that were technically able to walk. I looked perfectly healthy. But if I was being honest with myself, walking had become too difficult for me to do anymore.

I continued to experience mixed emotions, but as the night went on, I felt gratitude more than anything that I have a husband who doesn't shame me about lyme disease and all that has come with it, who makes me laugh like a kid again, and who made the most of what we were going through then. He is my greatest answer to prayer.

That summer, as I began using the wheelchair regularly, a part of me healed in that wheelchair. I was no longer in denial.

The wheelchair ended up being a tool that made my life a lot easier. And any time that shame would rise in me, I would be reminded of the words of one of my favorite people to listen to, Katherine Wolfe, said about her own wheelchair that she's been in for many years. She said, "this is my seat of honor."

It wasn't until I married Andy that I was able to be graceful with myself and be flat-out honest about the pain without being ashamed about it - and even then, I had to fight that shame. I had lived with so many different people over the past nine years, and nobody saw the suffering every day consistently like a spouse would. Going to sleep and waking up right next to someone that loves me unconditionally forced me to be honest about my suffering and opened the door for more healing in my heart.

Andy bears my burdens with me has undoubtedly revealed the heart of Jesus to me in new ways. Andy knows what it means to sit with people in their pain. He saw my suffering in ways nobody ever had before, and he spoke words over every part of me that rid me of the shame and denial I had carried for many years. I no longer had to work jobs with crazy hours to try to pay my medical bills. I could rest, and I could receive. I could love and be loved and not be abandoned or shamed for the parts of me that I had tried to hide for so long.

Visible Redemption

Maybe you don't see any tangible grace that God has poured out on your life these past couple of years. Maybe you can't think of anything positive that has transpired from your life out of quarantine. Maybe a caring spouse hasn't been a part of your story. Some of you may be divorced and didn't experience any redemption through your marriage. Or some of you may be married, but you just can't seem to land in a healthy, positive place with your spouse.

Some of you may be single and so over waiting for the right one. Some of you may be in a wheelchair, and it isn't temporary like it was for me. Some of you may be so sick in your body that even thinking about having a good marriage or any relationship for that matter seems impossible.

God has most certainly used my marriage to bring me healing and redemption in ways that would've never been possible without Andy. But, even as profound and healing marriage has the potential to be, marriage does not make you whole. Andy isn't my savior.

We aren't perfect, and we've hurt each other along the way. But if you have a man who loves Jesus - even if he's mad at God because of watching you suffer every day has become too much – that's what counts. And when he's down and in need of mending - which happens to everyone from time to time - our behavior as wives can help their hearts soften and heal. But the Lord has to be the one leading because I know that when I try to be super wife in my own strength, it never ends well.

Though ours or most marriages may look limiting or constrictive to the world, it has brought both of us more freedom in different areas of our lives. Andy's strengths complement mine, and vise versa. Marriage is for a greater purpose.

Even still, with two people who love Jesus coming together, marriage is no cake walk. You have to fight for it. I honestly wish I had heard more from people about how hard it can be at times. But even though it can be very hard at times, the rewards are rich.

There's nothing like being known and loved just as you are. It is an example of God's heart and sacrifices for us and how He chose us and still chooses us every day even though He doesn't have to. Marriage shines God's heart to the world.

If you are reading this and you are divorced or have had extremely traumatic experiences in marriage, I am so sorry. If you're single, I hope this part of my story is a testimony that even when you're chronically ill, or you feel unlovable, it is still possible to find a caring spouse. I share this part of my story to show the redemption that God has brought into my life through Andy.

CHAPTER ELEVEN

Finding the Gold
By Andy

Sharing the burden of chronic illness with someone is a very challenging task. You see the suffering of someone you love daily without knowing the remedy, you wrestle with a tumult of emotions ranging from sorrow to rage and wonder how or why a benevolent, faithful God would allow such tragedy. You find yourself at the end of your rope begging for mercy and seeking help from those around you but are usually left feeling judged and fatigued. Your sighs become heavier, your eyes tired, and dreams and hopes for your future seem smothered out like water over hot coals. And although all these things are real and painful, I have also found a depth and understanding like veins of gold in mountainous terrain. Some things that cannot be attained by the will of the flesh or knowledge, but only through experiencing revelation by the Spirit of God through suffering.

Character over Currency

I loved being Lauren's superman. When I originally creeped on her facebook page after scrolling through

"Laurens in Franklin, TN" looking for the familiar face of the girl I had just met, I found her and saw a posted fundraiser for the treatment she needed for a disease called Lyme. I remember googling Lyme and briefly learning about what it all entailed and how it affected someone. I did not ever feel anxious or intimidated by it because I was captivated by her sweet face. I welcomed the challenge to love unconditionally a girl I had just met. Cupid had hit me in the butt.

As we grew in our relationship, I poured myself out willingly and happily to see the smile it brought to her face and the joy it made me feel. As we dated, there was a unique connection that Lyme caused which drew us closer quickly. It's hard to hide oneself when you are forced to be vulnerable. We shared tears and laughter and kisses. Although we had pain, it was more bearable together.

Fast forward two years down the road. We are both exhausted, weak, and spent. The unconditional love that once flowed out of me so naturally had been replaced with a short temper, frustration, and blame. Although we reconciled quickly by the grace of God, the valiant young man who cupid shot was now a weary one. We struggled financially weekly, if not daily, we tried to seek affordable treatment that only left us in worse situations and usually Lauren in worse health, and walked in the shame of what others thought having to ask for help regularly. I thought I was patient. I thought I was steadfast. But my efforts paled to contend with Lyme. It would wake up before me, go to bed after me, and sustain itself longer throughout the day.

I believe God has given me a gift in patience and compassion - the rare ability to step into someone else's circumstances and empathize with them like it was my own. It was something I was proud of, and it brought me joy, but suffering helped reveal something to me that my own strength would have never. That even in the depths of my deepest love and service, I had a limit to which I could give.

SILENT SUFFERING

I thought I was patient until patience wore out. I thought I was compassionate until compassion left. I thought I loved well until the day I realized that my love was conditional. The day and night in and out of watching Lauren experience terrible suffering, trying my best to solve the problems, and being so ineffective brought me into a place of hostility. Not so much towards Lauren, but to God. I would lash out at God, regularly enraged by His permission to Lauren's pain. "Why would you allow someone you love to experience so much suffering? Why haven't you answered our prayers? Why isn't there healing when we've had elders anoint her with oil?" My arguments against God would mount, and my patience was gone.

As hard as it is to admit it, my patience came with a price tag. It came with unspoken expectations that would need to be met to continue giving at the current rate. It seemed so noble and admirable, but inwardly, deep in the darkest reaches of my heart, it was self-serving. It came at a price.

This is what God showed me, that I saw patience as a commodity, as currency, and not as He intended - as character. I thought if I did enough and did the right things, I would see the right results and be rewarded. I believed that if I did something a certain amount of times for Lauren that she would respond a specific way or change her behavior. That I was "helping" her, and in return, I would receive what I believed my efforts were due.

My love, patience, compassion, were not embedded character traits that defined how I approached life; they were my currency which I loaned to people on the expectation that I would get my return. It's a hard pill to swallow when God reveals that I am not patient. I remember the day the Lord spoke those words. Not in a demeaning way, just truthful and direct. I had spent half the morning trying my best to accommodate myself to the suffering Lauren was experiencing, but at this point, there was no hiding it. I was trying to help her to alleviate my own pain. I blew up on her. Saying how ungrateful she was, how

I am not appreciated, and that she can figure it out on her own.

Confronting God and His absence of help, He told me I was not patient. I felt rage, all the times I sacrificed, all the times I poured myself out, all the times, in my limited perspective, I saw God's faithfulness nowhere, and I was the impatient one?! But it was true. An inarguable truth that I tried to justify to God and myself. But in my heart, I knew He was right.

I later reconciled with Lauren and apologized to her, but what God spoke lingered, and His words pierced my heart. With teary eyes, I asked, God, what do I do? I'm trying my best. "I know my son". I asked, why don't you heal Lauren, He said, "I'm doing a deeper work."

The day will come when God wipes away every tear from our eyes. There will be no more pain or sorrow, for the former things will have passed away. But we will live with Him forever in paradise.

A lot of us have been conditioned to think we aren't enough. That we won't measure up, that we're too short or too tall, too big or skinny, too dumb or slow, unable to do anything right or be of value. On that day, God took what I thought to be one of my most redeeming qualities and showed me how shallow it was. A moment that, in my fearful mind, would be absolutely crushing, but wasn't, in fact, it was the opposite. God did not say I am not enough but instead showed me that Jesus was. God told me that He is already as proud of me that He could ever be. That in Jesus, I lack nothing, and I am complete. That His strength is made perfect in my weakness. And that I could never earn His love.

That which we manifest in the flesh, we must sustain in it as well. All flesh is insufficient, but Jesus is enough. I learned that my patience, compassion, and love were all a currency I used to prove my worth to God and place debts on others, but Jesus showed me that He is my righteousness, and I could never earn it. This was the gold that I found in this: that I cannot, but God can. And He longs to. But we must first see our own needs before we will visit the Doctor. We must know our limitations and conditions before we can truly appreciate the life Jesus lived and what He gave us.

We do not enter into the Kingdom of God on merit but through the perfect life of a Holy God, Jesus. There is more freedom in this than in all self-righteousness. I can now rely on the strength of the one who can sustain love and not try to change my behavior but allow an all-sufficient God to refine my character.

As I cash in my currency and place my faith in Jesus, He gives me what I need for the day to be the husband and support He's calling me to be. And although suffering still occurs and many painful days and nights, I paused, take a deep breath, ask Jesus for His strength, then endure with His patience and love through the hardships we face.

Better or Bitter

I have come to believe that suffering leads you into two places, bitterness or betterness, and the choice is yours. I remember when Lauren and I were talking with our close friends seeking marriage advice and counsel. After sharing how the pain of watching Lauren suffer led me to a place of anger towards God, our friend said there are only two options. You either get bitter or get better.

When I heard these words, I knew they rang true, although I wanted to have my frustrations vindicated in the moment. When you live with chronic illness or disability of any kind, you will feel out of control. You find yourself in a place where your will and desires are cut off from your ability to achieve them—placed in a desert without your consent.

But deserts can be a place of great growth and challenge. A place where you will be tested beyond your limits but where you will find a deep strength inside yourself as well.

I have always been a laid-back person, probably to a fault. I am happy to go with the flow of things and I'm naturally agreeable. I've been called a peacemaker but lean closer to being a peacekeeper because of my dislike of confrontation.

Throughout Lauren and I's first years of marriage, this was my goal, to keep the peace. If there was a need, I would happily meet it. If there was pain, I would do whatever I could to soothe it. If there was suffering, I could easily add a silver lining just to get myself out of the burden of what she was experiencing. Trying to will a smile and joy plastered on the face of torment.

At first, I was able to sustain this with relative ease. Although challenging, I could muster the strength to alleviate to the best of my ability. Somehow though, the things of more importance I missed, one of which being prayer.

I did not lead us in the right type of prayer. I definitely prayed, but it wasn't to ask God for strength, His presence, or perseverance, but to yield to this torment and take this burden away. That isn't a bad prayer. It is so important to ask God honestly for the desires of your heart, but when the Lord refuses to remove your thorn, to keep asking Him to do so can lead you into resentment, which is where I fell.

I've heard it said like this, bitterness leads to resentment, resentment leads to vengeance, and vengeance leads to the dark side. In my heart, I've teetered between resentment and vengeance with the Lord. I placed all my expectations on God to do what I deemed the right thing to be, which is to heal Lauren miraculously. Night after night and day after day, I would press Him with the same earnest request, not holding back, "please remove this ungodly, wicked torment from your daughter and fill her with healing. Now again, this is a good thing, a great thing, and I know the Lord will do it, but God does allow suffering for a greater purpose. And at times, unfortunately, suffering is the only motivation to get us moving when we've become complacent in our lives.

But what God did show me is that my prayers towards Him were to make my life easier, not to make us more like

Jesus, not to mold our character in men and women of God, not to be steadfast and long-suffering like our savior, but the quick fix, easy way out. This mentality will not help you through suffering. As much as wanting to alleviate the pain of someone you love is such a good thing and is God's heart and His plan that will, without doubt, come into fruition, asking Him to be our strength, hope, and friend will unequivocally be more helpful to you.

Reliance

I love the Lord's prayer, and I think most Christians do. There is so much power in reciting it out loud and in the quiet of your heart. But there is one thing, during this dry season that would frustrate me while I prayed it: "give us our daily bread." I happily recited this hundreds of times with joy, eating three hearty meals a day with weeks' worth of supply in our fridge and pantry, of course, but when the days came of uncertainty and the late nights thinking about what bills to pay, would we have enough for gas and groceries, and where are we going to live that's any kind of affordable and not moldy, these words were not a comfort.

I would look around at what everyone had, those Godly and ungodly, and be filled with bitterness. "Why would you give us so little when you're so big and capable?" "Why won't you give us a small, safe home we could call our own when you speak life into existence?" "Haven't we served you faithfully, and this is what we get?" Unfortunately, bitterness has the tendency to grow in dry places.

Although I asked God for my daily bread, when it came to having to trust Him for it, I was undone. Fear and anxiety would creep over me, and not just about our finances, but about what others would think. The thought of going without a meal was regularly easier than asking for money. That just filled me with shame, guilt, and judgment that was less tolerable. But through it all, God never failed to provide. We ate good meals. Although we had to choose which bills to be late on, we made our payments. The Lord even put loving couples in our lives who showed us grace when it came to paying rent. We managed to get treatment when we needed it.

But something greater than all this happened. The need for God alone to come through for us grew. Shaking at first, from "God will take care of us and has never failed us!" in the morning, to "how are we going to keep living like this and what are we doing!" in the evening. Gradually arriving to a more secure steadfast faith that the Lord has anointed our steps and He is trustworthy. He will take care of us. A gift that can only come through experiencing. Having to place your weight in the hands of a God you've never seen and trust again that He is good and loves you in the midst of terrible suffering. When I look up to my Father in heaven now, there is a relationship that is stronger because of dryness and weakness. Just like your daily bread, yesterday's trust for God won't be sufficient for today; it's an ever-growing process of trusting again and again.

I am stubborn and have kicked fervently against the goads, but God, in His faithful love, is teaching me how to trust the only reliable thing in this life or the next. Not food, not money, not other people, not health, but Himself alone.

Individuals Together

At this point, you may be thinking, wow, Lauren's husband has a lot of anger and resentment built up. Friend, it was a surprise to me too. But through all the hard laboring days, God has still brought us good friends, joy, laughter, provision, and beautiful moments.

I remember sitting in counseling with Lauren being told by our counselor that he likes to start with one person when doing marriage counseling. This made sense to me because Lauren has been through so much trauma. I was happy to support her through this. So naturally, when he said, "Andy, we will start with you," I was disturbed. I definitely have issues, but not like what Lauren's experienced. But begrudgingly, I proceeded.

It did not take long to get to the point of tension during our session—this being date nights. Now I love taking Lauren out and being intentional in our relationship, but up to this point, Lyme had manifested itself in all facets of our lives. I believed that my role as her healer was of more significance than that of her partner, and that the sacrifices I made in those areas, be it cooking, cleaning, massages, showed my affection towards her. But what Lauren needed wasn't a caretaker but a husband.

I had been in the role of caretaking to a degree in my life before Lauren, having a parent with mental illness. I developed unhealthy patterns through this. I would give and service with all I had to make one "feel" better to whatever degree that entails then crash. I would need to dissociate and disconnect from all people bearing the weight of their own pain and problems. I think this developed from an early age and trickled into Lauren's and my marriage as well.

When Lauren mentioned doing date nights in counseling, I was not happy. I felt the sense that "I give so much, and now I have to do more?" "Are you serious? Any other person would be grateful for how I served." But the truth was that Lauren was aboundingly grateful, but I had learned to give in unhealthy ways.

I always wanted to protect others from experiencing any pain. However, I could step in front of any physical or emotional pain to alleviate it's blow on the other would be my goal. I was good at this. But what I realized is that Lauren didn't want that. I could not stop the pain that she felt or cure Lyme disease but trying to keep her from any type of pain by any means necessary put unspoken, unrealistic expectations on her to respond in a certain way and prevented me from giving her what she really needed. So, when I learned that I was operating in an unhealthy manner as opposed to being loving, I felt ripped off and unappreciated. This is why date nights, a thing of unity and joy, became a burden to me.

God began to show me that my idea of what Lauren

needed wasn't always accurate. That although physical healing was our primary goal, we still needed to tend to our marriage - our relationship as husband and wife. That date nights were so important for us. Not just to get our minds off the hardship, but that we would continue to grow in love with each other.

Jesus loves relationships. He earnestly wants to have one with you and me. He also wants us to have one with each other. Doing fun, silly date nights seemed unimportant to me because the beast of Lyme was such a weight, but God in the midst of all chaos, still wanted me to pursue my wife and not just her healing. We must continue to make time for the things that don't make sense, trusting God with our other needs and pursuing meaningful moments with each other.

Music

We each have been given so many special and unique gifts. We tend to elevate some and minimize others, but God sees it differently. He does not withhold or value things the way we do. He made us as individuals. Each reflecting a unique aspect of His Glory for worship and serving our fellow man. He has put an unreplicated purpose in all of us.

What I found in our suffering was that my gifts and desires took a backseat. Now, this isn't uncommon, and there are times in our lives we have to lay down our desires for the ones we love, but the Lord was showing me how He wanted me to continue to pursue the dreams and talents inside of me.

This, like date nights, didn't make sense to me. There were bigger burdens and problems in front of us, and taking time to play music, a gift God has given me, seemed unintelligent. Yet, in God's perfect way, He managed to convince my heart with relative ease that this was His will for me.

Learning to take time for yourself may seem like the wrong thing to do. Satan will trick you into thinking you are being self-serving and avoiding responsibility, but God has a purpose for it. Not only is it a way to cultivate the unique gifts God has given you, but it's also a way to show God that you trust Him. That only He can tend to and heal a loved one. It will also help you from experiencing bitterness and resentment towards someone you love. There is meaning in your life beyond suffering. Trust God with the weight of suffering and take time to worship your Creator through your music, dance, art, workouts, sports, reading, writing, or just sitting on the porch drinking coffee.

We are a long way from the end of our journey. There is always another mountain and valley, victory and defeat. There are days when I tell God even if I was in the fire at a ten for the rest of my life, I wouldn't come close to being the person I long to be. Every time I turn the corner or think I understand what's going on, God does something new or shows me perspective on things I thought I knew. I am continually humbled, but eternally grateful.

If suffering only produced the heart in me that showed my all-consuming need for Jesus, it would be enough, but He does so much more than that. I've softened, strengthened, and have learned how to love others well. Through it all, God has been faithful to me. A friend said this life is like one grain of sand on an entire beach. Even if that grain was filled with horrible suffering, it would still be but a glimpse in eternity's eyes. Yet, God still shows His love to broken people in that grain and never leaves us. While playing the piano and writing recently, the Lord put these words on my heart:

Without hesitation He calls us by name, to walk on the water and stand in the flame and though it may linger my child brave the Lord will fulfill every word He will say.

To have faith in the midst of terrible suffering may be one of the most beautiful things a human being can do. To return to our Creator with trust in the indescribable pain is unique to us and will never again be attainable after we leave this world. But even if we fail and curse God in our pain, He loves us still. Even if we fail, it was never our efforts that God desired, but our faith in Him. Trust, again, amidst the storms of life and belief again that God is good and worthy to be praised.

CHAPTER TWELVE

Preparation

"He will yet fill your mouth with laughter and your lips
with shouts of joy. Your enemies will be clothed in shame,
and the tents of the wicked will be no more."
Job 8:21-22 (NIV)

Toward the end of summer 2020, Andy and I decided
to move from Tennessee to Colorado. There we were, in
our white Highlander with a small trailer hitched to the
back headed west. No jobs lined up. No home lined up.
Nobody we knew. Two naive kids, not thinking about
everything that could go wrong, just trusting and believing
that this was where Jesus was leading us. Keep in mind that
I'm only writing these words one year later, but for
whatever reason, we feel way more grown-up than we were
then.

We arrived in colorful Colorado on a sunny evening in
early August, having no idea where we would live. After
staying at campsites and Airbnbs, we ended up moving to
a town north of Denver. The couple we rented from who
lived above us were very kind when we moved in. They

invited us to all their family dinners on Sundays. They even bought us a big TV. Things seemed like they were making a turn for the better, and we were finally on our way to getting the quality of life that we had been yearning for back.

Then, I unexpectedly entered the deepest depression I've ever experienced. My heart began to feel weaker, and I experienced a sharp pain in it that became more frequent until it became constant. My hands, feet, and face felt numb and itchy everywhere, my neck and back felt broken, my brain in a thick fog and continuous forgetfulness. I had no idea how to help my body anymore or my brain for that matter. That winter, it was as if I was sleepwalking through life and utterly exhausted during the moments that I was awake.

Before moving to Colorado, I dreamed of living in the mountains and being healed. I guess I thought that with moving to a place with better air quality and a fresh start, I'd be doing way better. I thought I'd be working full-time again. I thought I'd get my life back again. So, when that didn't happen, I was disappointed. The logic behind that dream may not make much sense, but for me, the little dreams and hopes along the way are what keep me fighting.

As time went on, it became apparent that my health would be worse whenever I would be in our home, and it got to the point that I preferred sleeping in our car more than in our home. There were open doors in that home to a lot of demonic activity. Andy and I have never experienced anything like it.

It also became apparent that my gut needed more repairing. Parasites had been wreaking havoc on my gut and health for God knows how long, and had never been adequately addressed or treated. I wasn't dealing with just a few minuscule parasites, but literally, hundreds that I excreted through my bowels. I lost count after 200. And I don't mean microscopic ones, but worms that had grown up inside my body (most at least an inch long and some many inches long). Yes, I know it's disgusting, but this is the reality for many people who are chronically ill: parasites are never properly addressed or treated, gut health remains poor, and people remain ill.

One night, in the middle of my never-ending parasite cleanse, I got rid of about 30 worms at once. And due to the amount of toxins being released, I was having dark and unstable thoughts.

Something about fighting for your life for so long changes the way you see things. Your eyes open to things you couldn't see before. During this season, I became highly aware of the spiritual realm. I realized how much of a spiritual war my health battle had always been.

During that time, Andy decided to take me to the ER because of the continual pain in my heart and vertigo to the point where I wouldn't be able to move my head in any direction for periods at a time in bed. I felt paralyzed. They told me nothing was wrong even though there were clearly problems I was having that their machines were picking up on – I get it, it's an ER. They aren't equipped to help lyme patients.

Andy and I ended up moving out of our home. The hardest part was that when we tried to end the lease early, the Christian couple we were renting from didn't believe anything we told them. They mockingly suggested that it must've been because of the color of the walls that I couldn't live there.

It's been a year since those experiences took place. I'm still healing. I also went through a deliverance during that season, which I highly recommend to people with chronic illness because they often don't realize that there have been curses spoken over them or that witchcraft is being used against them - which is all very real. At one point during my deliverance, the whole house shook and roared. It was traced back to my great grandfather, who was heavily involved in demonic activity.

Walking through chronic lyme this long has taught me countless lessons like how a lot of life is about acceptance and that not everything is spiritual, nor is everything that we see as it is. One of my friends with lyme was told by a neurofeedback specialist that a certain part of her brain was operating at 2%. Lyme and trauma affect your brain so much! That's very important to address. There are many studies by different doctors all claiming that a very high percentage of autism, MS, and dementia cases are traced back to spirochetes in the brain. Lyme hides itself for being what it is, but eventually, people will see how much it truly is the root of so many health issues.

What's been beneficial to me is taking lots of high-quality omega 3s, eating bison (which has consistently been fantastic for me and my blood type over the years – as well as venison and elk), sheep cheese, and butter from Europe, moving my body even when it feels broken, breathing techniques, lymphatic drainage techniques, and doing everything I can to take care of my mental health in the process of healing.

If you want more advice, I've written out some tools in the back of this book that have helped me. I had the privilege to work with wonderful practitioners who educated me along the way so that I'd know how to handle many different problems on my own. But I can still get tripped up.

God is the One who brings transformation and healing. You can think as positively as possible, try every tool and supplement out there, but that doesn't sustain you when you feel like you're no longer human. Jesus does. You can eat as healthy as you possibly can, but that doesn't compare with the bread of life.

Light Breaks Through

During that process of going through a very intense spiritual battle, by the grace of God, light broke through. Right in the middle of my darkest night. Slowly but surely, God began bringing me new visions, new dreams, new goals, deeper purpose, and a desire to live my life to the fullest again.

I became a certified IV technician because I know firsthand how helpful nutritional IVs can be for someone who is chronically ill. Unfortunately, I couldn't commit to the job that I wanted because the reality was that I wasn't well enough yet to show up to a job every day. Most days, I was still stuck in bed.

God kept coming through, though. A kind man who has his own fitness and recovery center in Denver offered me to use his infrared sauna whenever I needed to for free, which was a massive help to us financially and was a tremendous gift in my healing journey.

Then, we met Brian and Kendra - through a dog-sitting app out of all places. After we dog-sat for them, they invited us over to hang out. As we shared a little of our story, Brian and Kendra said how they didn't realize the severity of our situation or the fact that we had been nomads all over the state of Colorado for the last three months. I promise, it sounds way more adventurous than it was. It was insanely stressful and challenging.

Brian and Kendra offered us to stay with them free of charge while we were still paying rent at our old home that we weren't living in. We have no words to describe what Brian and Kendra did for us. They helped us gain some of our dignity back in some of our most embarrassing times. They didn't go to church, yet they showed us the love of Jesus better than people in the church were at the time.

We ended up living with Brian and Kendra in their guest room for over four months. They were kind to us when we felt like burdens, and they didn't show judgment towards us and our situation. We're still friends with Brian and Kendra and their two Boxers, who are our favorite dogs in the entire world: Darla and Bernie.

The Tides Are Changing

There's a different kind of closeness to Jesus that happens when you're walking through fire day in and day out. It isn't blissful, but it's real. Every time I'm at the end of my rope, there's somehow still more hope and endurance to be found in the presence of Jesus.

On the last Sunday in December 2020, my friend, Jess, preached a powerful sermon at her church. She talked about how sometimes our breakthroughs don't look the way we expect them to.

At the end, she invited anyone to get baptized if they wanted to. I was humbled when God put it on my heart to get baptized again that day. The last time I had been baptized was when I was nine years old – ironically, the same year that lyme came and changed my life.

It wasn't anything fancy, just a big tub outside. The water was cold. But this time, as I stepped into the water, fully aware of what I was doing, I was declaring my need for Him. I was asking for a fresh baptism of whatever He wanted to do in my life. I got the feeling that night that hell was trembling at the unstoppable work of God that continues to happen and the healing that is going to burst out of these bones.

After my baptism, I went on a fast where the Lord convicted me of many things. I flushed all my pharmaceutical drugs and the medications I had for the "just in case" moments down the toilet. That's just what I felt I needed to do. Then chronic guilt, something that was tied to my illness, reared its ugly head. I felt so guilty for not contributing financially to our family during that season, and it was eating me alive.

Since then, it's been a daily choice to grow in self-awareness. I can now catch myself much more quickly when I am operating in guilt. Then because I am aware of it, I can give it to God and ask for His grace to enable me to do what He's called me to do - and no longer carry any guilt about any of it. I realized that the voice of chronic guilt I was hearing was a voice I had grown up with, and I was done hearing it. It's a process, and God is the one who enables that process, but what I can say is that getting free from chronic guilt is incredible.

It has created so much space inside of me to cultivate creativity and not feel like I'm doing anything wrong anymore. I never knew how much freedom would be in this space. Although guilt still rears its ugly head from time to time, God's grace enables me to let go of it as he reminds me who I am.

After my fast, I entered into a season of repentance. For walking into places that maybe God was never leading me to go in the first place. For taking antibiotics and other drugs that maybe God was never leading me to take. For giving into lies.

Then I repented to the Lord for saying that I didn't want to live, and I felt a flood of compassion pouring out over me from my Father. I sensed Him say, "you don't have to repent about that, my child." I sensed Him grieving with me the fact that I had been denied basic needs for so long and needing relief so much to the point of despair.

It isn't that I didn't want to live; it's that I didn't know how to keep living like I was living after barely getting by for so long. I was a human who didn't feel capable of handling any more pain. I couldn't handle watching my husband go through hell as he watched me go through hell and his health fall apart while I myself was just trying to survive. Andy nor I could imagine sustaining in a life filled with suffering that showed no relent. We both had such an overwhelming feeling of wanting to die and didn't know how to deal with it.

There's so much I want to say regarding this. I want to tell whoever is reading this who has also not wanted to live or is maybe even contemplating suicide now that they are so irreplaceably valuable. That it's worth it to stick around. That God loves them. That God's not upset with them for how they feel. That they don't have to feel guilty or shameful for having the desire to not live anymore. That this isn't a taboo topic, and that so many incredibly respected people have gone through the same thing. That God carried Andy and I through our most painful season, and by His grace, we chose life.

"I will not die but live, and will proclaim what the LORD has done." – Psalm 118:17 (NIV)

Here are the words I wrote in my journal this morning: "The tides are changing." Not sure where it came from, but each word hit the paper with grace and certainty. Somehow, I find assurance in these words. Somehow, after the thousands and thousands of prayers, after the thousands and thousands of days that I never want to relive, after all the unanswered questions, there will be light. The tides will change, and we will finally be able to breathe.

The Power of Relationship

I wanted to share the revelations I've had over this past year in this chapter, but I think if I did, I'd be missing it. You see, we could gain all the tools and knowledge in the world, but where would that lead us without Jesus?

This morning as I was sitting on the porch of where we're currently dog-sitting, with my bible in my lap, as I struggled to get into the word, God spoke identity and encouragement over me. He wasn't waiting until I got everything figured out or until I read four chapters; He just wanted to be with me. That love and fellowship that He pours out on me drive me to want to know Him and seek Him in His word more.

You can look all over scripture and what you'll find as you read through the pages is that it's a roadmap. Its pages are bursting with revelation, wisdom, and life. There are keys to unlocking some gold in our deserts in those pages.

God has given us an abundance of promises in His word. There is a miraculous power in speaking those promises out loud. I believe that He also sometimes gives us specific promises over our lives straight from His heart.

Sometimes when we don't see those promises fulfilled, we get confused. But maybe God is doing something in and through us that our children or generations after them will fully reap the benefits of. As we walk in faith, as we believe and speak out the promises of God from His word: we can't even begin to comprehend the ripple effects to come. We may never see those ripple effects, but that's not the point.

The people of Hebrews of 11 did not receive the things promised to them; they only saw them and welcomed them from a distance, admitting that they were foreigners and strangers on the earth. Abel, Enoch, Noah, Abraham, Sarah, Isaac, and Jacob all continually put their faith in God even into their old age when they did not get what was promised.

"All these people were still living by faith when they died. They did not receive the things promised; they only saw them and welcomed them from a distance, admitting that they were foreigners and strangers on earth. People who say such things show that they are looking for a country of their own. If they had been thinking of the country they had left, they would have had the opportunity to return. Instead, they were longing for a better country—a heavenly one. Therefore God is not ashamed to be called their God, for he has prepared a city for them". - Hebrews

11:13-16 (NIV)

It's all so much easier said than done, but what if we started giving Jesus more of our time, hearts, and devotion? Not just coming to Him when we are desperate or scared but coming to Him at the crack of dawn, when we're joyful, after a victory, or when we think we've got it all figured out on our own?

Sitting with Him because He's worthy of our time. Talking to Him about what's hard because He shares in our cup of grief. Keeping our eyes fixed on Him. Because what I can say is that relationship with Jesus is our greatest weapon. He speaks identity over our insecurities, He pours healing water over all our wounds, He speaks grace where we need it most. He loves us when we feel unlovable.

What if we took Him at His word? What if we believed everything He said? What if we let Him take our hands and lead us out of the pits we find ourselves in because He's the only One who can?

What if we believed that God to carry us through? What if we believed that we are fearfully and wonderfully made? What if we weren't crushed under the unbearable weights that have been put on us? What if we sat in the presence of God and He took the burdens off of our shoulders?

I'm finding all over again that the answer to my problems lies in sitting with my King. He may not give me every solution to my problems, but He lightens my load. He guides my steps.

Some who read this may be frustrated or brush it off because we haven't seen Jesus come through the way we thought He would. Because the pain is too deep, and we're hurting too much. Because we feel abandoned. Because we don't see any evidence of a good God around us. I know.

But when you sit with Him, when you linger in His presence, change happens. The changes typically look subtle, but those changes can mysteriously alter the course of your day, your week, and your life as you keep getting His presence. All the weights and pressures that were once so worrisome get lighter, and our perspectives shift.

So, I don't share all this to say that Jesus has come and fixed all our problems. No, in fact, this past year felt like the complete opposite. I'm not going to BS you and say that everything's great or that life is easy by any means because it's not.

I got angry a lot last year. I like to think it was all righteous anger about what my body was going through and how hard our lives have been, but I'm sure if God told me all the nasty things that are still inside my heart, I'd realize that the anger is not all righteous. I'd also like to think the anger has only been expressed alone with God in my car in the thick of the pain, but it has also been expressed in front of my husband and even towards my husband in my worst moments.

God reminds me that I am a new creation. That He has cleansed me of yesterday's sins. That His mercies are new every morning and that every day I have a choice. That I can choose to embrace my life in all its messiness. That I can give my anger to God so He can replace it with love and self-control. That I'm an imperfect human with an infinitely amazing Father who can redeem the ugliest and darkest situations.

Andy and I have lived in Colorado for over a year now. On the real: our first 365 days felt like complete survival and a breaking inside us that we never imagined experiencing - the kind of breaking that happens in your soul through suffering that doesn't go away. But that breaking has allowed all our mediocre Christianity to be sifted out of us until all that remains is something real.

We still haven't seen the promises God has spoken over us fulfilled yet, but here we are, still standing. Still believing that God is working in our lives. And you know, I think all this is preparation for what's to come. I know when we do see the promises fulfilled and the suffering has ceased, we will be so much more prepared than before.

Some seasons you may feel isolated, betrayed, angry, misunderstood, alone, sad, jaded, and exhausted. Don't give up. Don't lose heart. You will be vindicated.

We live in an ungodly world, and if we're going to pursue holiness, we shouldn't expect it to be easy. It may feel excruciatingly lonely and grueling at times, but all the "greats" in the bible went through similar things. Those trying times were their seasons of preparation.

I believe that I'm in a season of preparation. It doesn't feel pretty, and I can't wait for it to be over, but I know I'll be glad I went through this season when I look back on my life. I know my children will be better off because of it. I know God will use it.

On the days I've been filled with faith and on the same day have been completely faithless, and yet His love has remained steadfast. His love has kept me alive.

As much as my pride wants to go against this truth, I'm finding all over again that Jesus is the remedy. And although the world tugs, although fear gnaws at my ears and pain presses me beyond my capacity, they cannot stand against the voice of the One who loves me better than anyone can ever love me.

Chronic Illness Reveals Who Your Friends Are

Many seasons of my life, I've found myself staring out of windows wondering, "how do I engage with the world anymore?" I can fake not being sick, or maybe, just maybe, I can show up just as I am.

The only answer I have for myself now is grace. Exponential grace and self-compassion. If people want to be my friend, they will make efforts. I won't have to wonder if they care about me.

Don't push yourself. Don't deny the reality of your life. If people are mad you don't visit, that's not on you.

There is a time for everything. One season you may be filled with joy, and another, you may be depressed. One season you may have energy for relationships, and another, you may not. Don't push yourself beyond your capacity, and don't guilt yourself for not giving when you have nothing to give.

The older I get, the more I am concluding to not push my body in a way that puts me in denial about what I go through. Yes, it's very healthy to get out and to be in community, but don't fake not being sick to the point that I did for so many years. You forfeit being seen, and you can't form legitimate relationships with people because they don't fully know you, only the counterfeit face you put out every time you are around them.

Most people don't know how to treat people with chronic illness. Forgive them. How can they understand when what you go through is invisible, and you don't know how to share what you're going through?

Many people would rather paint a silver lining or give more advice instead of listen. They'd rather send their friends who are hurting a verse or a bible study instead of step into their pain and ask what their friends need from them. They're happy to be a part of your painful reality until it starts costing them something.

Then there are the few golden ones who are willing to step into suffering and carry the burdens with you. When you're running on E and have nothing to give, spend time with your golden ones.

I've seen a common theme over the last decade. That theme has been my friends with lyme being looked at like they're crazy. One of satan's many tactics is to make people feel like they are crazy, and I believe that tactic is rampant in the chronic illness community. It's too hard for people to believe the truth of the matter that their friends are going through something that can't be logically explained.

If you love someone with chronic lyme, you know that it's hard. If you plan on being in someone's life who has chronic lyme or another life-altering health condition, know that it's going to be hard. It will cost you something. You will have to choose to believe what they're going through, have grace, and have patience. But love is never wasted.

Belief over people's silent suffering is the determining factor if you're going to be a part of their healing journey or not. Eventually, your unbelief over their suffering will drive them away from you, and they won't trust you anymore.

If you have health issues and the people around you don't believe what you're going through, set boundaries with them. Then find people who do. You need people who believe you and are cheering you on in your journey.

Learning From a Pixar Movie

We live in a crazy time. Many people aren't thinking for themselves anymore, and yet our God-given brains and intuition are so powerful.

Our greatest weapon is knowing God's love. The enemy doesn't want us hearing from God because hearing Him and being in relationship with Him is what transforms us. So, if you haven't heard it before, satan is after your relationship with God. He doesn't want you knowing your identity in Christ. I don't share this to induce fear, I share it because we need healthy spiritual awareness in these days.

In a day in age where fear is being thrown in our faces every day, we still have a choice to not make our personal decisions out of fear. Like the scene in the movie, WALLE, where Wall-E doesn't follow the track that's been set in place for all the other robots to never step foot off, we can be the ones that get off the track that everyone else is on. We can still do simple things like get in the dirt, use our brains, look in the eyes of those we love, dance, dream, hold hands, and seek after the truth. Those simple rhythms can lead to changing so many people's lives, like Wall-E and Eve did.

God does not operate out of fear. "For God has not given us a spirit of fear and timidity, but of power and of love and of a sound mind" (2 Timothy 1:7 NKJV). We don't have to operate out of fear. And remember, don't base the success of something off the immediate result. Sometimes you may feel like you're in a deeper hole, but it's for a greater purpose.

In the end, Jesus wins. To be accurate, He already won. He's coming back, and it's going to be epic.

Darkness will not prevail, my friend. Sickness will not win. God will sing songs of deliverance over us and will proclaim a shout of victory over all these very real and, at times, unbearable trials that you and I face.

CHAPTER THIRTEEN

I See Miracles

"Heal me, O Lord, and I shall be healed; save me, and
I will be saved, for you are the one I praise."
Jeremiah 17:14 (NIV)

Last year, during a Good Friday service, we heard a woman named Piper preach on suffering. It was probably the best sermon I've ever heard on suffering. I recently asked Piper for her sermon notes, and as I'm looking at them, I'm overwhelmed at choosing which snippets to share with you because everything was so good. Here are a few things she said:

"We are often tempted to forsake the process in favor of the miraculous, but then we'd miss the fullness."

"Jesus was a carpenter. Carpentry takes precision and attention to detail. It requires process."

"Jesus didn't ask us to fellowship in His suffering without first fellowshipping in ours."

"He fellowshipped in our suffering. He lost people he loved – notice Joseph is not mentioned in Jesus' ministry because he likely died when Jesus was between the ages of 12-19. Jesus was the first born of his house; he was the one that all the responsibility fell to once Joseph was gone. He was familiar with the burden of caring for a family."

The day after that service, while I was alone at home, I lost my temper. I was in pain, having difficulty controlling the movements in my hands, and was worn out from it all. I was tired of trying to put on a face that said, "I'm okay." Then as I sat on my shower chair and washed my hair, I wept in a way I hadn't in a very long time. It was a way that I knew was good for me.

As I thought about all the words I'd written in this book, I grieved the fact that I still wasn't healed like I thought I'd be. Lyme had caused an enormous physical, emotional, and mental burden on us, and there was so much mending to take place.

Andy came home in the middle of my grieving and graciously loved me through the pain and tears. We went on with our days, and God gave us joy as He typically does on the more challenging days. The next day was Easter. As the day progressed, my ability to walk regressed.

What do we conclude? Do we dare to believe that He's still good? Do we dare to keep living our lives fully present through all the pain and grief and desires for our lives to look completely different than they do in real life? Well, I do because I'd be foolish not to by now.

Easter is the beginning of God's restoration to all things. The resurrection of Jesus is a constant reminder that even death does not have the final say. So, I can go on with my day knowing that lyme is not the final word. God will restore me, and He will restore Andy. "We are hard pressed on every side, but not crushed; perplexed, but not in despair; persecuted, but not abandoned; struck down, but not destroyed. We always carry around in our body the death of Jesus, so that the life of Jesus may also be revealed in our body" (2nd Corinthians 4:8-10 NIV).

We are going to face trials in this life, that's a given. Only by the grace of God and the same power that rose Jesus from the grave - that resurrection power that lives inside of us - is going to get us through our darkest nights. "I also pray that you will understand the incredible greatness of God's power for us who believe Him. This is the same mighty power that raised Christ from the dead and seated Him in the place of honor at God's right hand in the heavenly realms." – Ephesians 1:19-20 (NIV)

We carry the power of His death and resurrection.

Through all the trials and triumphs, God has been with me. On my weakest days, He has manifested His strength in supernatural ways. He's been sending angels to my side, He's refreshed me, and He's carried me through the thousands of days when I was too weak. He's used hardship to change my heart and show me new dimensions of His character.

And even if God allows this thorn in my side to stick around longer, I know He's using my most challenging days more than I realize.

The days that I've had a hard time walking have humbled me. Those days made me rely on God's strength radically more. They reminded me of my desperate need for my Savior and that I can't do this on my own. And because of all those hard days in bed, the days where I've been able to get out and live more of a "normal" life are lived differently. I don't take them for granted.

The days I've woken up and haven't been able to get out of bed because of how much pain I was in was an invitation to grieve, give myself permission to not be okay, and to keep growing in grace. My pulse tells me that I'm still alive, and there are still many things for me to do here on earth, even if those things look so different from what I expected.

Despite the aches and scars and crazy state that our world is currently in, God is still moving. He's moving in the church. He's moving in His people. He's using suffering. I continue to pray and plead to God for my complete healing, but in the waiting, He keeps healing my heart and soul, and He keeps restoring my dignity.

But, you know, it isn't about getting my dignity restored. It isn't even about my rewards in Heaven. It's about seeing and knowing God. It's about looking back on my life and knowing that He hasn't forsaken me. It's about sharing that with others so they can see Him in their stories too.

He's still fighting for you, and for me even in all the wails and groans when we're all alone. He's using tribulation to make us stronger in our spirits even when it doesn't feel like it at all. "Endure hardship as discipline; God is treating you as his children. For what children are not disciplined by their father? If you are not disciplined—and everyone undergoes discipline—then you are not legitimate, not true sons and daughters at all." - Hebrews 12:7-8 (NIV)

I've been trying to wrap this book up for a long time, all the while I didn't recognize the miracle that was taking place all along. What God has done in me is a miracle. What He has done in Andy is a miracle.

I'm prone to be a selfish, impatient, judgmental, and prideful human being. Yet God's grace and love enable and empower me to overcome and be transformed in my heart. He allows me to change at the heart level, which is a miracle. Growing in grace for myself, my husband, and those around me while suffering in this kind of way is a miracle. Growing in love is a miracle.

Andy has his own story to share about the trauma he's gone through. People who take on such a demanding role need healing, too. They need restoration over their minds, emotions, and hearts too. The pain of a spouse helplessly watching their loved one suffer day after day is a pain that I can't understand nor fathom.

I'm learning how to understand the one who had to take care of me better. I'm continually learning that the way I love him and pray for him can be a massive part of helping him mend and heal. God is the healer, He does the work, but if I choose to partner with God every day, my husband can benefit greatly.

When Andy and I were growing up, neither of us ever imagined our lives to look anything like they have. We didn't imagine waking up every day to a suffering that is lonely and brings countless challenges with it. But the enemy will not win. Jesus already won. We are victorious. We will see true victory, and we will see healing that's beyond this world.

We're growing in kindness and wholeness. We're praying differently. Prayer is a lifestyle and lifeline. We're continuing to learn how to cope and heal from the traumatic toll that lyme has taken on us individually and on our marriage.

We're rebuilding, which takes *time*.

"My goal is that they may be encouraged in heart and united in love, so that they may have the full riches of complete understanding, in order that they may know the mystery of God, namely, Christ, in whom are hidden all the treasures of wisdom and knowledge."
Colossians 2: 2-3 (NIV)

I'm growing in knowing God's love. Not just in my head but in my heart. I'm seeking out the hidden treasures to be found in His words and His eyes.

Years from now, I know that chronic illness will be nothing but a faint memory. It will be only a tiny part of our story. And in the meantime, we are still growing into the people I think we were always meant to become.

We yearn for the day that we have a bunch of kiddos running around our kitchen who never have to suffer like we have. We yearn for consistently good health. We yearn for me to wake up without a pain that has become all too familiar.

I believe one day that will happen, and maybe I'll write another book about it. But I think the miracle here is that we still believe. We still choose to worship God. We haven't lost hope. We haven't lost faith. Andy wrote these simple words recently as he was moving our stuff out of our old place, and I thought they were too good not to share:

I see a new light falling on me
I had no hope in my eyes but now I can see
What was planned for my fall has been turned around
To make me look like my Lord and for jewels on my crown

I wish we all had even more understanding as to why God permits suffering, but the words in His book of life give me plenty of my daily bread and stories of others whose weaknesses amplified God's strength. I don't doubt that any of them regret any of the times that they looked to God in their pain, and I don't doubt that they've been richly rewarded for their faith in God ever since they stepped foot into eternity.

The jewels on the crowns of those of us who have suffered will be worth it. The miracles He did in us will be worth it. The ways He used our suffering will be worth it.

To still thoroughly believe that God is good is a miracle. To still be alive is a miracle. To still pray for the people who have hurt me is a miracle. And to hear, "job well done, you suffered well" from the only One it matters to hear those words from will make this all worth it one day.

I've been trying to make sense of the last decade of my life as I've written this book, yet I sense God saying to me this morning, "you don't have to make sense of it. I'll show you my miraculous power. Sit back and watch what I do." So, I'm sitting here today, hands wide open. I'm setting myself up in a posture to receive again. I'm praying audaciously, and I'm walking a little taller. Not striving, just believing that He's not even close to done with me. He's not even close to done with you.

CHAPTER FOURTEEN
Breaking Cycles of Trauma

"Lord, what are human beings that you care for them,
mere mortals that you think of them? They are like a
breath; their days are like a fleeting shadow"
Psalm 144: 3-4 (NIV)

For months, this book sat on my computer, thirteen chapters completed. I knew the book wasn't quite finished, but I didn't know what else to write. I kept sensing to be patient and not publish the book yet, but I didn't understand. Then, I began to see glimpses of what the greater purpose was.

We found a unique home out on a country road with open fields and a view of the mountains that make you feel like you're in Switzerland. In the upstairs loft of the house is a quiet stillness surrounded by natural light and pine trees hanging out outside the windows. We immediately moved in. It was the first time we had our own place in over a year.

The amount of progress I have made in these few short months has been nothing short of phenomenal. When we first moved into our house, I was experiencing the worst pain in my brain that I had ever experienced. My central nervous system felt utterly hijacked. My brain was stuck in a trauma loop and didn't know how to get out. But God.

Unresolved trauma hides in many different forms. For me, it hid in illness, anger, depression, toxic thought patterns, among other adverse outcomes.

Many people who are stuck in trauma don't realize that they are stuck in trauma or how to get out, for that matter. Many see fewer possibilities in store for them as time goes on. Their self-esteem is low, and their perspectives become more limited.

I'd always known that my body and brain had been stuck in some sort of trauma. Retraining your brain, seeking out help in many and sometimes odd forms, and creating new memories have all been incredible tools to help me mend, but that never-ending feeling of doom was still there underneath the surface. Lyme most certainly plays a role in that doom, but lyme is tied to trauma, making one massive mess.

Lyme is the same frequency as fear and abandonment, while parasites are the same frequency as trauma. So, if you grew up in trauma, fear, and abandonment, toxic feelings probably feel natural to you. Your brain remembers these patterns.

It can feel like a never-ending cycle trying to get free from the effects of trauma. For years, I did what many stuck people in trauma do: I self-sabotaged myself much of the time and thought that people were typically out to get me. I thought people wanted me to fail. I had many friends at different seasons of my life, but after so much trauma and not feeling like people cared (another feeling many who are stuck in trauma feel), I realized two years into marriage that I had very little trust for humans anymore, and the only person I trusted (most of the time) was my husband.

So, I decided it was time to dive into my trauma. I started seeing two counselors – one to do EMDR with and another to emotionally process with.

I also finally found somewhere that took our insurance and did neurofeedback. I know someone who completely went into remission from lyme due to neurofeedback, so of course, I wanted to give it a try! Andy and I are both about to start.

As I began to dive into the trauma, God began changing my thoughts. There's power in learning to sit in the tension and then relax in that tension. There's power in learning how to silence your inner critic.

I began to feel empowered in ways I never have before. And then, slowly but surely, trauma began to leave my body. It happened some days like a tiny flicker and others like a flood, and at 28 years old, I was healing.

Many days, I felt a tingly and warm feeling in my hands and feet – a good feeling, a feeling that I wasn't used to. All the places in my body that had been numb or in pain began to come back to life.

EMDR did not help me, and after reading Annie Hopper's book, Wired for Healing, I began to understand why. I came to learn that I had a limbic system impairment. This needed to be dealt with. So, I spent four days doing nothing but Annie Hopper's DNRS Bootcamp DVD program. In the introduction, she asks if we as participants would commit to spending at least an hour a day doing the exercises for a minimum of six months. I was all in. What did I have to lose? I had spent the last decade of my life trying to get my life back, so a minimum of an hour a day felt like a cakewalk to me if it meant it would help me get my life back.

Just before starting DNRS, a major issue arose in our environment. Andy and I began to smell gas any time we would go upstairs, and it was especially strong whenever we would get near our closet in our bedroom. Turns out there was a gas leak. At this point, my cognitive state and mobility were at a very low state, and it took everything in me to get out of bed.

Our landlord and her son made it clear that they could've cared less about our well-beings through the process - what's up with hardhearted landlords?! They were more concerned about their pipes freezing when I was nervous about turning the furnace back on because of how badly it had affected me and the fact that it very well could've killed us had I not insisted on getting someone to come check on it. The same day that the gas leak was fixed, my symptoms improved. And they continued to improve as time went on.

Then, I went to see a lyme specialist who had been highly recommended to me. She was empathetic, and I liked her. I wanted to do testing, and I voiced that multiple times during the appointment, especially with mold, to see what to do next to treat it. As the appointment progressed, everything was rushed. After an hour, she gave me some homeopathics and sent me home. For everything, I spent $499. The next time I was scheduled to see her was nearly three months later.

This is not uncommon for lyme patients. They often feel unheard and misunderstood. They struggle to create a positive relationship with some practitioners who don't take the time to try to understand the entire situation and properly test the patient in order to evaluate what needs to be done.

Andy reached out to her assistant, explaining our concerns and asking that we get me back into the clinic for testing sooner than later. Her assistant took over a week to give us any answers.

The reality is that there are many situations and circumstances outside of our control. But what if we shifted the focus onto only what we could control? There are so many tools in front of me I can use to continue this healing process. Health practitioners can guide me, but they can't rescue me.

I am going to see that specialist again next month. And I know that I will keep healing. And because I'm no longer living in mold, chronic stress, on top of so many blockages (emotionally, mentally, spiritually, and in my environment) while getting treatment, I will finally get into remission and live a life that is foreign to the very sick body I used to have.

Sometimes, you have to fight for what you need. Sometimes you have to speak up. Other times, you have to get quiet with yourself and God and do whatever that thing is He is calling you to do. Because no human will care for your body as much as you can or advocate for your health like you can. Our bodies are God's holy temples, so there is a responsibility to take care of them. So, we do what we can, not forgetting to rest in Him, knowing that His grace will carry us through whatever trials we face.

This 10-year long process has been exhausting. It has required so much patience. But it has changed me. I'm proud of who I've become in the process. And I'm humbled. Nothing good in me or in my story has come from me. It's all been God's doing.

Back to DNRS. Annie Hopper's approach and personal story shows how incredibly life-changing neuroplasticity can be. I began the DNRS program on December 11th, 2021. She asks that you set aside four days dedicated to DNRS when you first start. The first two days, it was challenging for me. I saw and read stories of people who had become paranoid and had PTSD from different products that they couldn't tolerate, and I began wondering if this was the right kind of program for me. I felt like many of the practices Annie was asking us to do were things I was already doing to a degree. It was a bit of a kick in my pride to really give DNRS a shot, but I'm so glad I did. Because although my impairment may have looked different than others, I still had one.

Breakthrough is an understatement to describe what DNRS has and is doing for me. This past decade of my life consisted of a pattern. The pattern went like this: For moments, hours, and sometimes even days at a time, I'd be functioning. People would look at me and consider me "well." I'd be operating at high levels and working very hard, trying to make up for lost time. Then I'd crash.

Since finishing DNRS and continuing the practice daily, my life has changed. I'm no longer crashing. I don't have to pay for the days that I did what normal people do.

Every day, as I continue to repeat patterns to let my brain know that it's okay to relax now, as I continue to remind myself that I am calm and capable in every situation, I'm becoming a stronger force. A few weeks ago, I cleaned my house for two hours nonstop. And I mean cleaning, like scrubbing floorboards and all the gross crevasses. And then the next day, no crash. Or the next day.

Sometimes I catch myself running up and down our stairs like it's nothing. Other times, I realize how much more at ease my body is than it was even two months ago, and I'm blown away.

There are still trials. But the way my brain and limbic system respond to them has changed. I don't have to freak out.

Covid came for a visit this week, which has been no fun. But it shows me just how far I've come when my immune system is fighting this thing like a champ and I'm able to take care of my husband whose case has been worse than mine.

DNRS has helped me so much. It has taught my body how to come out of fight or flight mode and not see everything as a threat. I see covid as just another thing that is strengthening my immune system. I do what I can to take care of myself, stick to the regimen of supplements and herbs that have been super helpful, and leave the rest up to Jesus.

I'm learning that my brain can create new pathways. I'm learning that my associations with words and experiences matter. I believe we have the power to change our associations. We have the power to alter the state of our brains, which in my case, is transforming my health.

I've learned how to live in tension, and now I'm learning how to thrive in that tension. Yes, this is possible!

Healing Is a Process

There's still work to be done. We are still healing. Community is certainly a part of this healing like it always has been. I believe this journey towards wholeness is ongoing, full of twists, turns, speedbumps, lessons, and growth.

Everyone will have their own opinion of what they think you need to do. Trust yourself. Trust what you need. Your self-intuition is powerful, and you are strong.

People won't always understand the battle you're facing or the amount of strength it's taken for you to be where you are today. People may not show you any respect. Don't let these petty things get to you. You're on your own healing journey. You are growing in your calling and mission in life.

As I spend quiet days here in our new home that's surrounded by chickens, cows, and coyotes, reflecting on what was and turning my attention to what is to come, I am thankful.

Genuine gratitude goes an infinitely long way. Gratitude makes me more aware of the beauty all around me. Gratitude allows me to see the wide variety of vibrant plants all over the garden of God's heart that I'm engulfed in. Gratitude unlocks more of the blessings along the way.

"Therefore, as you have received Christ Jesus the Lord, walk in Him, rooted and built up in Him and established in the faith, just as you were taught, and overflowing with thankfulness" - Colossians 2:6-7 (NIV)

I've got a card on my fridge from my aunt and uncle with their adorable kiddos on it. It's nothing formal; it's just four of them being goofy little kids. One of my cousins has her mouth wide open with a popsicle in her mouth. On the bottom of the card, it says, "in all things, gratitude." This card was sent out right after my aunt delivered a still-born baby. The card that I walk past every day reminds me that we can all find gratitude in any and every situation.

I'm thankful for all the moments I've shared with you. I hope that in sharing them with you, you know that you aren't alone and that your suffering matters to Jesus. I hope you see that there's always a reason to keep going. All the painful, hilarious, scary, exhausting, mundane moments of your life are not to be quickly disregarded or forgotten. They make up a marvelous tapestry of clay called you and me that the Potter continues to mold.

This is life, my friend. Whether there's a valley or a mountain peak before you, be sure to live it. Even in suffering and illness that feels unbearable, we still have breath in our lungs, a chance to love the people in front of us, and a chance to make a difference in their lives. You and I can embrace all the contrasting moments of life, even the scary ones, knowing that we don't have to fend for ourselves because God's working on our behalf and working things out for our good.

There has been immense pain, loss, opposition, and oppression that my friends and millions of others have experienced, beyond horrific to put into words. I'm not solely talking about lyme disease patients, who obviously need more help and for their illness to be properly recognized and treated, but what is happening all around the world every day. People are hurting.

Like a crisp morning where the sunlight is piercing into your eyes and causes a smile to break out on your face, God is still yearning to shine His light on you and I's weary souls.

We need Jesus now more than ever. Some of us keep searching for something out there in the world that makes us feel more complete, but we already know in our spirits what, or more accurately, whom we need. The place where our journeys gain true meaning, depth, and goodness is with Jesus. What an honor it is that He still chooses to sit and commune with you and me.

Joy Is Coming

"For the revelation awaits an appointed time; it speaks of the end and will not prove false. Though it linger, wait for it; it will certainly come and will not delay" - Habakkuk 2:3 (NIV)

I guess it was never about arriving, but about becoming. This mile marker in my life is one that I celebrate. I'm glad I took the time to reflect on the race I've been running and who I've become in the process. I had a multitude of you show up at some mile marker along the way with food, money, clothes, or literally a roof over my head, cheering me on, telling me to keep running. I didn't understand your generosity, but you motivated me to keep running and not give up.

Truly, all there is to show are stories - moments of God invading my little world. Every mile marker where I hit a wall, and the world would say, "give up already," God came in and gave me a double portion of His love and strength. In my weakness, His power was truly made perfect; it was evident and undeniable, forcing me to see that He is faithful. He is holy. He is God.

In your own race that is set before you, embrace the mud that splatters all over your legs. The views. The times when the breeze refreshes you. Embrace the people running around you. Embrace who you're becoming. Also, embrace the silence. The times when you don't see anyone in sight and are so weak about to fall to your knees, and the only thing that keeps you going is the voice of the Shepherd. Embrace those times because they are sacred.

One day, God met me alone in my favorite foggy woods in Nashville. It was a rainy afternoon, I was tired, but I knew the Lord was calling me to go on an adventure with Him. I quit second-guessing and contemplating and went. As I breathed in crisp and cold Tennessee air and heard the sounds of rushing water behind me, God was teaching me through a herd of eight deer in front of my eyes. The seven others were following the head of the pack wherever he went.

I was reminded again that obedience is what matters. Not good deeds, or what others think we should do. I was also reminded in those woods that the Lord's love and goodness is a never-ending river, full of new life. That He desires good things for our lives. That to know His voice, His gentle and kind whispers, and to follow them even when they seem foolish - are everything. Every season is a season... which means it must end. After all the suffering, there is a new season of wonder, enjoyment, delight, and refreshment coming for you and me. Jesus is the One who brings the healing. What is learned in the suffering is invaluable; it's pure gold.

Whenever He decides to completely heal me and all my friends who suffer, whenever He restores what has been lost and stolen, to Him be all the glory. In the meantime, He's changing us.

This story is still being written and would not be possible without the selfless souls in my life. Chronic illness has not been lost time, rather a time of refining and learning. I haven't suffered without purpose, and neither do you. Amid all the pain and defeat I have seen God do so many miracles, and I now know that it's a waste of time to doubt that He cares about all the details of my life and yours. He is making our feet more like the feet of deer as our steps become more sure-footed, and He is granting us holy water to drink as we are led beside the quiet waters. Our weeping may last for a night or thousands of nights, but I assure you that joy. is. coming.

This is just the beginning. I hope that what God has done in my life so far touches your heart and inspires you to trust Him more. He is worthy to be trusted and praised.

You aren't alone, my friend. Your life is valuable, and you. are. priceless. Don't let anybody tell you differently.

Now, this isn't the usual way to end a book, but if you are willing, there is one thing I ask of you now. Put this book down and be silent. Kneel, sit, lie down - put your face on the floor if you want. Wherever you find yourself today, simply be with Jesus and breathe. Quiet your soul before Him. Come back to the heart of worship. Because when all else fails, He won't.

Then Jesus came to them and said, *"All authority in heaven and on earth has been given to Me. Therefore go and make disciples of all nations, baptizing them in the name of the Father and of the Son and of the Holy Spirit, and teaching them to obey all that I have commanded you. And surely I am with you always, to the very end of the age"...* -Matthew 28: 18-20 (NIV)

What Has Helped Me

If you have lyme, I'm sure you've found that works for one person may not work for another. So, I am not saying any of these will help you, I'm just sharing what has helped me!

- Obviously DNRS by Annie Hopper! You can buy her program at retrainingthebrain.com.

- Infrared Sauna (I got my own at home which actually helps me sweat more than the wooden ones I've been using for years and doesn't overheat my head which is a gamechanger! I wish I got it a decade ago! The brand is SereneLife - $200 on amazon).

- Liposomal glutathione (Quicksilver brand) – this helps me so much with energy and cognitive function. It's been proven to help with lyme and dementia.

- Ozone (putting it in my ears and nose helps me a lot)

- Enemas (I have the Aussie Health brand and use SA Wilson's gold roast premium coffee) and colon hydrotherapy (Angel of Water system)

- Diatomaceous earth (the benefits are endless)

- The HBOT (hyperbaric oxygen chamber) has been extremely helpful to me at times with brain fog, pain, and energy

- Cryotherapy for inflammation (Groupon many times has deals at least here in the Boulder, CO area)

- Nutritional IVs (pricey, but so helpful if you can ever afford them)

- Mimosa Pudica Seed (this is what has helped me get rid of parasites more than anything else)

- Formula 1 by Microbe Formulas (cellcore's sister company that doesn't require you to be a health practitioner to buy their products unlike cellcore) has been the second most helpful in getting rid of parasites

- Plexus products - the slim drink was one of the most beneficial things that helped me have the energy to start working again last summer and have also helped with my menstrual cycle a lot too. Vitalbiome and biocleanse has also helped me a lot. I could not tolerate probio, even when I opened the capsule and put a tiny in my water. I think it might be best that people with severe mold illness should steer clear from that before starting treatment with a doctor.

- Eating low histamine foods (for mold illness)

- TUDCA by Microbe Formulas (Microbe Formulas is Cellcore's sister company and you don't have to be a healthcare provider to buy their products!)

- Gaba by Quicksilver

- For sleep: SleeptThru by Gaia and Truecalm by NOW ...And although I know it isn't the best for you, Benadryl sometimes take the edge off lyme symptoms and helps me fall asleep fast!

- Worship

- And don't forget to breathe! ☺

Helpful Resources

- Toxic by Neil Nathan (book)

- Wired for Healing by Annie Hopper (book)

- The Tick Chicks podcast:
- www.thetickchicks.com/podcast

- ILTWYL (I Love The Way You Lyme): my friend Michaela's nonprofit. She has raised money for over 20 lyme patients to get treatment this past year alone and is doing so much for the lyme community even though she herself is still struggling so much. For more resources, visit www.iltwyl.org. You can also find her nonprofit on instagram: @ilovethewayyoulyme.

- Emily Morrow. Emily is a Jesus loving practitioner who has shared so much helpful information with the world! Her website: Bio.site/emilymorrow

Thank you for reading my book!

I hope you enjoyed *Silent Suffering*. If you found this book helpful at all, could you please leave an amazon review? It's very hard being a new author, especially when you're self-publishing. Reviews are super helpful!

ABOUT THE AUTHOR

Lauren is a voice of encouragement, support, and empowerment for people who are battling chronic illness and don't know where to turn for help.

Lauren enjoys hiking, kayaking, creating community, and making a difference in people's lives. Lauren lives on a country road in Colorado among chickens, cows, and wildflowers with her husband, Andy.

Instagram: @lomurph93
Facebook: https://www.facebook.com/lauren.stoll.52

Made in the USA
Las Vegas, NV
02 April 2022